C0-AUZ-716

TheBackbencher

TheBackbencher
Trials and tribulations of a Member of Parliament
GordonAiken

McClelland and Stewart Limited

McClelland and Stewart Limited
The Canadian Publishers
25 Hollinger Road, Toronto

0-7710-0056-1

Printed and bound in Canada

Contents

INTRODUCTION

When I was ten years old, rattling along coach class on the train to Toronto, I had my first contact with greatness. There was, it seemed, a Member of Parliament riding in the parlour car, on his way to Ottawa. Curiosity got the better of me. I struggled through the lurching cars to the rear of the train, and peered through the glass door. Sure enough, there he was, impossible to mistake. Reclining easily in a plush swivel chair, he was reading a newspaper, puffing now and then on a big fat cigar. He was wearing a black striped suit, the open waistcoat revealing a gold watch chain crossing his large stomach. As he raised his arm to summon the porter, a flash of light reflected from the jewelled cuff links in his starched white shirt. The parlour car seemed to be floating along on another track, as it bore this prominent person to his functions in the capital. Not daring to disturb him, I turned and went back to the coach, dreaming of the day I might achieve such eminence.

George Drew didn't think they were all that eminent some years later, as he waited for the Chairman to restore order. It was May 15th, 1956. The Canadian House of Commons was in an angry mood. C.D. Howe had ridden roughshod over the House with a harsh motion on a pipeline bill, calling on the massive Liberal majority for support. They had complied without question. When the Leader of the Opposition got up to comment, they expected a blast. And they didn't have long to wait.

For his part, Drew was furious. This group of "honourable members" had gone along with everything the government proposed. Not only that, they had been insulting while they did it. No shame-faced or hesitant supporters they. With loud applause and banging of desks for their champions, and hoots of derision for the opposition, they had crushed all resistance. They reminded him for all the world of trained seals. They responded to their masters on signal. Their hands pounding on their desks looked like the flapping of flippers, and their hooting sounded like seals barking. And as Drew began to speak, they drowned him out. Chairman William Robinson restored order, and Drew rose once again.

"Now that the trained seals are silent," he began sarcastically, and shouts of protest were raised.

Once again the chairman intervened. He did not consider "trained seals" an appropriate expression to use.

"Perhaps," he suggested, "the Leader of the Opposition might withdraw those words."

Not a chance. Drew had chosen the least offensive words he had in mind, and he had no intention of withdrawing them. So another argument started over that. But when the day was over, the expression had become established in the language of parliament. "Trained seals," repeated a New Zealander the following year in his House of Representatives. "Trained seals," Canadian Members began to fling across the Chamber, as they pointed accusing fingers at servile opponents.

When I was elected to the House of Commons on June 10th, 1957, I didn't really identify with the grey eminence I had seen on the train in my youth. That was a childhood impression of an era far past. Nor did I identify with the trained seals of 1956. They had been wiped out. Those days of arrogant behaviour and servile compliance were gone. I belonged to the new breed of politician, product of the modern generation. Of course, I was a party man. And I had campaigned in my leader's name, so I had to acknowledge his direction of affairs. I was a member of the government team. But I felt that these things were a background within which Members could exercise their free will. I struggled with this illusion for a couple of years, justifying, making allowances, accepting small victories. But then one day, I had to admit it. I was a trained seal too. What's more, I was called one.

It happened because I had decided to master the rules and take part in the debates. Ready to make a speech at a moment's notice, I was often asked to talk on private member's bills. It was something of a game to talk them out beyond the allotted hour, so they couldn't come to a vote. On one occasion, when I got up to stall things, someone in the opposition called out: "Here come the trained seals."

The trained seals didn't disappear in 1957. Nor in 1963 when the government changed again. They had new names, new faces, new ideas. But it often looked like the same old act on the same stage. Players moved in, did their act and moved out again. Every election brought a new crop of hopefuls, bent on putting things right. But first they had to find out what was wrong, and by then many were conditioned to accept it.

But don't form any hasty conclusions. I want to take you for a light look at some of the people and some of the situations they run into. When we are finished, maybe you will know a little better what you do to them when they are elected. Are they still trained seals like the ones George Drew saw in 1956? Or aristocrats of the seventies, riding planes instead of trains? You may be surprised.

THE CANDIDATE

"I'm ready, willing and able"

As the Cunard liner *Carinthia* ploughed her way westward from Europe, the rugged hills of Canada's east coast appeared one morning with the dawn. The early sun cast a golden glow along the tops of the wooded hills in their fall colours, leaving the rocky shore in ominous darkness. Something exhilarating about this rough landscape challenges the spirit of conquest and adventure. Newcomers and returning travellers alike for over three centuries have seen behind those endless hills a summons to make a new start. I had this feeling, too, as Marie and I watched our native land tower into view on returning from Europe in September, 1956. "I am waiting," the country seemed to say. "Do something."

Reluctantly leaving the morning freshness, we finally went down to the ship's lounge. A new issue of the "Ocean News" was placed on a table, and the first item caused my heart to skip a beat.

GEORGE DREW RESIGNS AS CONSERVATIVE LEADER
SAYS PARTY MUST MAKE A NEW START

A new start. The very words that had been running through my mind. Today I want to be part of it. I had considered being a candidate for election in Parry Sound - Muskoka, but the nomination meeting was only two weeks away. We made a quick decision right then. By noon, telegrams were radioed landward in which I announced my candidacy, resigned as Family Court judge and advised riding president E.P. Lee. The die was cast. And at the convention in Burks Falls on October 11th I won, by just 20 votes, the approval of my party to be its candidate. Nine months later, I was elected Member.

What about the other Members? Who are they, and how did

they get there? I have seen six new groups arrive, and no two stories are the same. They seem to spring up at random from among their fellows, as though touched by fate with a magic wand. They are different in essence from hundreds around them. There are others just as well qualified. But somehow these chosen few emerge for a time from among eighty thousand others, to become the instrument of local and national public affairs; without preparation and without training. Then sooner or later they return to the multitude from which they came. And while thus brought forward, some are touched by the extra glow of cabinet appointment, public acclaim and brilliant performance. They, like others, cling briefly to the tokens of office, and are swept away by the same fate that brought them there.

Why one person is chosen and another rejected, why one steps forward and a better holds back, is without logic. Their special appointment to tamper with the lives of their fellow man derives in some way from sheer desire and the ability to win. Yet something special brought each one to his place. It is not always brilliance. It could have been tenacity, good luck or even dullness. Not ordinary dullness, mind you. That would get him nowhere. It had to be unusual dullness; of the type that could brand a person as single-minded.

The first hurdle to cross is the nominating convention, called by each political party when an election is imminent. Conventions are conducted according to the tradition of the organization. They may be classed as dangerous, safe and half-safe. An open convention, where everyone present gets a vote, is dangerous. There has been less inclination to hold them, especially in the Hamilton area, since the first time Ellen Fairclough was elected in 1950. She was nominated early and had an enthusiastic group of young Conservaties out working. The Liberals had a strong candidate lined up too, and it promised to be a real race.

The Liberals had an open convention. There was an excellent turnout and the officials weore than pleased to see a large number of young people scattered among the crowd. "We can give Ellen Fairclough's gang a run with these kids," said the chairman of he meeting. "They really look eager."

In addition to the favoured candidate, a couple of others had let their names stand to make a contest of it. The first ballot brought a surprise. One of the other candidates showed up strong. Thinking he must have some hidden qualities, people began to switch over to him; and on the final ballot he won. There was consternation on the platform. But there was no backing off; the convention had chosen.

"Well, let's get the names of some of these young people and put them to work," said the chairman to those around him. But the eager young people had drifted off. Most of them were young Conservatives, who had never realized politics could be so exciting. Having chosen their opponent, they went out to beat him. And they did.

The safe convention is a delegate convention. This does not mean it is safe for any particular candidate, but it cannot be packed by outsiders or any one candidate. The credentials are handed out in advance to party representatives in each subdivision. They are the only ones who can vote.

But there are those who say the delegate convention is undemocratic. It keeps the "old gang" in control and others lose interest. So the half-safe convention was devised. Everyone who holds a membership card can vote.

This holds other dangers. A prospective candidate and his friends can sell memberships to all who will support him. They can even throw in the membership fee. It's a cheap vote at the price. Once the sale of memberships gets going, the opposing faction catches on, and they start selling too. On February 28, 1972, John Morison, three times elected as Liberal Member for Halton-Wentworth, went to his nominating convention all ready to do a repeat performance. But some of the party members thought otherwise, and they put up Norman McGuinness against him. It was a membership convention. The sale of memberships had suddenly spurted, and by nomination night over 3000 had been sold, twice as many as at the previous convention in 1968. Obviously John didn't get his share, for he was defeated. And, incidentally, so was Norman McGuiness on election day.

A nominating convention serves several purposes. The main objective, of course, is to choose a candidate. But it is also an excellent place to line up poll captains and works, and to set up the lines of communcation for the campaign. It is likewise a good place for a candidate to meet the rank and file of the party. An experienced candidate will refuse to get drawn into conversations, photography or interviews at the end of the meeting. He

12

will be at the door, with his wife, meeting everyone who was there.

Above all, the meeting serves as a morale builder for the coming campaign. People need pepping up if they are going to work. They have to be convinced that a government formed by the other party would be a disaster. They have to be assured that they have a good candidate and leader. They must leave the meeting in a fighting mood. For this reason, it is cusomary to have well-known party men speak at nominations and early meetings. For the main speakers it is a real strain travelling around a large country like Canada.

George Hees is one of the most popular guest speakers. He is effective and good-natured and butters everybody up in fine style. To help him over the rough spots when there is little time to eat or sleep, he always takes a lunch, a blanket and a pillow. He is particularly careful that his driver knows where he is. His caution comes from an unfortunate incident in October, 1957. He was on his way to speak at a meeting for Sidney E. Smith, the University of Toronto president who had just been appointed Secretary of State for External Affairs. At that time, George was federal Minister of Transport, in charge of air, rail and land transportation in Canada. As he was snoozing in the back seat, his driver stopped at a service station to go to the wash room. George woke up when the driver was gone, and decided to go for a little walk. The driver returned and assuming that his passenger was still sleeping, drove off without him.

Time being short, Canada's number one transport man decided to hitch-hike. A car stopped and asked him where he was going. "I'm George Hees, and I'm trying to hitch a ride to Norwood to speak at a meeting for the Foreign Minister," he explained.

Assuming the man was either drunk or crazy, the driver took off into the night without opening the door. After several cars passed, a truck driver finally recognized him and drove him to the meeting. Arriving at Norwood an hour late, George was telling what happened to the people standing around. They couldn't believe him either. "We know you're a busy man, Mr. Hees, and we're awfully glad you came," said one old-timer, "you don't have to make up a story for us."

Anyone seriously considering federal politics in Canada should belong to a political party. It is very easy to join. In fact, he will be welcomed with open arms. If he indicates any interest in working, he will put on the executive or even made president in no time at all. This gives him a good solid base from which to develop support.

It may be that the sitting Member comes from the same party. That can be a disadvantage, but it isn't impossible to defeat him at the convention. There were two such upsets in 1972. Two weeks after John Morison was defeated in Halton-Wentworth, Harry Moore lost his bid for renomination in Westaskiwin, Alberta. Harry had been a good Member too, but he had mentioned several times that he might not run again. They took him at his word, and nominated Stan Schellenberger, who later won the election.

It is not legally necessary to join a political party, but if you don't, the odds against winning are high. In the past 15 years only four Members have been elected as independents. Three of them, Speaker Lucien Lamoureux, Roch Lasalle and Maurice Allard were first elected as Members of a party and ran as independents in later elections. The fourth, J.A. Mongrain, classed himself as an independent Liberal. Party affiliation provides the candidate with workers to put up posters, address envelopes, arrange meetings and knock on doors at election time. Other incentives may be financial assistance and a red hot leader on whose coat-tails he can ride to victory.

There was one Canadian who made it on his own — or almost. At an election rally in Temiscouata, Quebec, there was a little man at the front of the hall who was asking for the floor. As the official speakers droned on, attention occasionally strayed towards him.

But when the introductions were finally completed, the candidate himself spoke. He read letters of commendation from many important persons, and finally his clincher, a personal letter from Sir Wilfrid Laurier. People nodded in satisfaction. But even as he spoke, word passed around that the man up at the front was Pouliot, who had been defeated at the nomination. He wanted to say something to the meeting. Why would they not let him speak? There was a buzz in the audience, and the officials became anxious. Why not let Pouliot have his few words? An independent had no chance in Temiscouata. So he was invited to speak.

Jean François Pouliot, Member of Parliament, rebel, Senator, then began 45 years of public service from the platform of his

14

opponent. He had failed to obtain the Liberal nomination. He could not get a crowd for his meetings. He had no backing and little money. But his message was simple. He told that meeting he had the courage to fight for Temiscouata in Parliament. "I have only one letter of recommendation," he added, "and that is from His Holiness, the Pope. I have it here in my hand. I did not hear my opponent read one from His Holiness."

In 1924 that made a lot of difference. On election day Pouliot headed the polls.

"The people of the riding really voted for His Holiness," he told me many years later, "but it was Jean François Pouliot who came to Ottawa."

For most people, defeat at the nomination is the end of the road for that election. They accept what is decided. Pouliot was different. But there were not many like him.

From the first moment a person has the stray thought that he might run for Parliament, his self-training begins. He starts moulding himself to the pattern he thinks appropriate. He becomes more pleasant, more accommodating. He talks to people he wouldn't otherwise tolerate. He spends more time in public. He has noticed that people vote according to the way they feel about a person. Not that he is efficient, or intelligent, or capable, but whether they like him or not. Other things being reasonably equal, the "real nice fellow" gets elected and the "sour puss" is sent back home. In one sense, this is good. It is good for the candidate. He becomes a little more human. It is good for the public — they have one less grouch around. But it is the thin edge of the wedge. It has started the compromise that can lead to sealdom.

Only those with very strong wills resist the temptation to bend a little in their attitude. And for them, the reward is generally defeat — at the convention or at the polls. A few obstinate people get elected: Ralph Cowan is one example. Elected for York Humber in 1962, he retained his gruff, grumpy approach unaltered. He said what he thought. He stood firm on his own beliefs. He laced into family friend Lester Pearson without mincing words. And his eventual reward was expulsion from the caucus of Liberal Members and later rejection as a candidate.

Everyone has an equal opportunity at a convention, but not

everyone has an equal chance. Tradition and human reluctance have placed obstacles in the way of some candidates. One of these is parachuting. Brigadier-General E.M. Leslie had one of the shortest serious candidatures in history. And that is not surprising, since he had a lot working against him. For one thing, he ran in a rural area where he was not a resident. For another thing, he didn't leave himself much time. He announced his resignation from the Armed Forces on a Monday morning, to seek the nomination the following night. Finally, he underrated the locals.

"I like the area and the people," he said generously, "they're the type who call a spade a damn shovel and won't be pushed around."

He was right. On Tuesday, September 12, 1972, they gave the Liberal nomination in Parry Sound - Muskoka to local resident Allan Knapp. But being a local wasn't enough, anyway. Knapp lost the election seven weeks later to Conservative Stan Darling.

Parachuting was invented long before aeroplanes. Politically it means a non-resident dropping into the riding from elsewhere to run for office. In general terms, local voters don't like it. There is something of a challenge to local pride if they cannot produce their own man. The parachute candidate is the stranger coming into the local society. He may not understand them. In modern transient society the attitude is mainly imaginary, but it is there. And it is a handicap.

In large urban areas the handicap is minimal. A resident of metropolitan Toronto or of Montreal, for example, could run in any of the city ridings, and few people would even think about it.

Parachuting was often practised in Canada's early years by party leaders. Sir John A.Macdonald, member for Kingston, Ontario and a native there, ran and was elected in Marquette, Manitoba after his home constituents unkindly rejected him in 1878. Later he was elected for Victoria, B.C. Not only that, but in 1882 to make sure he would not be defeated, he ran in two ridings, Carleton and Lennox. He was elected in both. He chose Carleton. In 1887 he had another try at the old home town of Kingston, but taking no chances he also ran in Carleton. Again he was elected in both. This time he resigned Carleton and was back as Member for Kingston.

Sir Wilfrid Laurier practised the same kind of parachuting. In 1896 he ran in his home seat of Quebec East and also in Saskatchewan riding, the predecessor of Prince Albert. He was elected in both, but resigned Saskatchewan. Though his tenure was brief, this riding was thus represented by three Prime Ministers, Laurier, King and Diefenbaker. On later occasions also, Laurier was elected in two seats. His prudence paid off in 1917, when he was defeated in Ottawa, but elected in Quebec East. The handicap of parachuting is minimal for party leaders. Tommy Douglas, when leader of the New Democratic Party won in British Columbia after defeat in his home province of Saskatchewan. Running in two seats simultaneously is no longer allowed in Canada, though it is still practised in some other countries, Norway and South Africa, for example.

There is little danger in parachuting into controlled territory, either. Prior to 1968, it was perfectly safe to float into most Newfoundland ridings. All one had to do was get the nod from Joey Smallwood, and the nomination and riding were assured. Canada's best-known parachute Member was Jack Pickersgill, a native of Ontario and Manitoba, who was handed the Newfoundland riding of Bonavista-Twillingate in 1953. He represented it for 15 years. His attitude toward his adopted province and riding would make most candidates shudder.

"Mr. Pickersgill," asked a reporter in the summer of 1972, "now that you are leaving public life, have you any plans to live in Newfoundland?"

"Oh, no," replied the long time cabinet minister, "if I got elected six times without living there, I see no reason to live there now."

Parachuting doesn't always work in Newfoundland. Max Keeping, Ottawa broadcaster, ran against Minister of Transport, Don Jamieson in Burin-Burgeo, Newfoundland, in 1972. Although he put up a good fight, Keeping was "creamed" as the expression goes, three to one. Of course, his cause wasn't helped much by giving his address on the ballot paper as R.R. No. 3, Metcalfe, Ontario.

There are other handicaps in trying to gain the nomination. Canadians have a strange streak called "loser rejection." They feel that a person who has run for office and lost, has had his chance and botched it. Someone else should have a try. In other countries, politics is considered something of a profession. The public may reject a candidate's ideas this time and accept them next. But in Canada, it's different. For one thing, the candidate often takes his defeat personally, and wouldn't run again if it was handed to him. For another, the party wouldn't likely hand it to him.

Pauline Jewett, when a political science teacher at Carleton University, made a study which showed that candidates in Canada, once defeated, are seldom later elected. This did not deter her personally, for after a defeat in 1962, she ran again in 1963 and was elected. But she was defeated in 1965. Undeterred, she changed parties in 1972 and tried again, and was defeated again. All of which must have proved what she already knew. Even former Members, once defeated, have less than an even break when trying again. In 1972, out of 10 who had already established their reputation, only 4 won after an intervening defeat — Alvin Hamilton, Heward Grafftey, Elwood Madill and Alex Patterson, all Conservatives.

There is another handicap in reaching the starting gate for an election. That is being a woman. Trying to assess the reasons has always been a favourite preoccupation. There are statistics and opinions unlimited. A Royal Commission on the Status of Women spent nearly four years travelling in Canada for public hearings on the position of women in Canadian society. It received 468 briefs, heard 890 witnesses and did voluminous research. In its 1970 report, it blamed local party brass for not giving women a break:

> It is at the constituency level. . . that disparagement of women candidates and the belief that a woman candidate will lose votes are usually encountered. Women who have been successful at the polls confirm that winning the nomination is a more formidable hurdle than winning the election.

But perhaps women are not really that interested. Grace MacInnis, the only woman Member from 1968 to 1972, believes that the great majority are not involved because they are not interested. She thinks this comes from recent pioneer tradition that women's proper place is in the home, and from an educational system which trains girls for a passive role.

There is another factor which holds down the percentages. Women are suckers for lost causes. They will jump in and accept a nomination nobody else wants. If they can't get party support they will run as an independent without a nomination. They work from the heart. In the 1972 election, only 4 of the 69 women candidates were nominated in ridings where their party then held the seat. All four got elected. Of the other 65, only one was elected, and that was Flora Macdonald. Hers was a triumph of hard work, good organization and personal attractiveness. Margaret Daly, Toronto Star staff writer, quoted a women's organizer on October 21, 1972 as saying:

> Things haven't changed. Most of the women running for all parties are serving the same purpose they've always served — to be sacrificial lambs in ridings that their party doesn't expect to win anyway.

Women in one category have almost always been successful in obtaining a nomination. They are widows of deceased Members, who contest their husband's vacant seat. These women have substantially boosted the total number of women elected in Canada. But they do not stay long. Jean Casselman from Ontario, Margaret Macdonald from Prince Edward Island, Isobel Hardie from the Northwest Territories, Eloise Jones from Saskatchewan and Margaret Rideout from New Brunswick were all elected in seats formerly held by their deceased husbands. I knew them all, and they are all very capable women. Jean (Casselman) Wadds was re-elected three times on her own personality and ability. The others soon dropped out, finding the life unsuitable. Some, like Jean Wadds, run because politics is in the blood. In 1972, Peggy Thatcher, widow of the former federal Member and Premier of Saskatchewan, got the nomination in Regina East, but she lost the election. Finances are no longer a factor: pensions are now provided for widows of deceased Members. If they run for office in the future, they will have about the same chance as other women. And that is not very good.

Party nomination is only the first step towards election in Canada. It gives the candidate the chance to run the main race. No one opposed George Doucett in the August 1957 federal by-election in Lanark, Ontario, but acclamations are extremely rare. Voters generally have a choice of two or more candidates. In many of the new African countries, and in most of the Communist countries, on the other hand, successful party nomination means you are in.

Only one political party submits names for election; and only one name is put forward. The representatives are considered to be democratically elected; and it has not been any push-over. Each person had to make the list, one way or another. But with the nomination, it is clear sailing all the way. For Canadians the fight is only starting.

The party which gives a candidate his chance can take it away at the next election. The local association doesn't ask too much. In return for the nomination, they want their Member to support the party. The connecting thread seems small enough at the time.

But when choices must be made later betweeen a Member's judgement and party decisions at any level, the thread can cut tightly. I found this myself in 1965 when I joined those calling for re-assessment of Mr. Diefenbaker's leadership. Many thought I had denied the party, and were very angry. But I held that leader and party were not identical, and the majority agreed. A Member, nevertheless, has an obligation to his supporters. And they hold an enforceable covenant from him. If he doesn't like the connection, they can sever it and cast him adrift.

Right at the beginning of his career a candidate voluntarily accepts a limitation on his freedom of action — a debt to his sponsors.

THE CAMPAIGN

"Knock on every door —"

The door opened just a fraction, and the woman inside peered suspiciously at two men on her doorstep. She had almost ignored the knock. But curiosity got the better of her and here she was, staring at two absolute strangers.

"Well, what do you want?" she asked without trying to conceal her annoyance.

"My name is Egan Chambers," explained one of the visitors, offering a card, "and I am running for parliament." "I might have known it," snapped the Irish matron. "I don't trust any of you politicians. You're all crooked."

The campaign manager glanced with amusement at his candidate. Blond, eager and looking younger than his 32 years, Egan Chambers didn't seem much like a Montreal politician in 1953.

"But madam," Egan protested, "I am really very honest, and I am new to politics."

"Never mind," replied his skeptical listener, "you'll catch on."

As the door began to swing shut, the manager knew something had to be done quickly, so he spoke up. "Think about it, madam," he urged. "Even if what you say is true, it will be years before this young man is as crooked as those other fellows."

The door stopped suddenly as the thought struck home. She half smiled, nodded and then snapped the door shut.

Egan Chambers never knew whether this quick thinking won him a vote or not. Many calls are wasted. But it is absolutely true that candidates who want to be elected in Canada must get out and knock on doors.

I learned early that personal communication between candidate and voter is important. It doesn't have to be anything profound. It only takes a few seconds. It's looking another person in the face and acknowledging that we are both doing our best. A few words, an understanding response satisfies him or her that I know what's going on. Otherwise, I am just a name on a piece of paper or a face on a poster. It is easy enough to swing in when everything is favourable. But you are on your own when the tide turns. That's when personal contact counts. I came by one of my most enthusiastic and constant supporters in a very brief encounter.

One spring day in 1958 I was making election calls near Sprucedale. Arriving at a farm gate, I looked up the long, wet laneway to a hilltop house. I could never drive it. After a moment's hesitation, I took out on foot. Slipping and struggling up the hill, I finally made it to the door. It opened immediately to my knock, and there stood Emmerson White, his wife and son. They had been watching from the moment I stopped the car.

"Not many people try that lane this time of year," he said, and the others nodded in agreement.

I didn't recognize his comment then as an expression of total acceptance of a guy who made a special effort. But it was. And he became the kind of supporter every candidate and Member dreams of: respected, sincere and outspoken. I had taken those extra few steps for him.

Election campaigns are ordeals, and the hardest part of most Members' existence. Yet they have their moments of humour, and the stimulation of human encounter. From the experience of grinding hard against the fabric of life, a more understanding person emerges.

A new candidate is deluged with things to do. He knows the external sign of election — road posters, radio and television appearances, meetings, newspaper advertising and pamphlets. But suddenly the magnitude of the organizational effort hits him. Workers must be recruited. Speeches have to be prepared. Meetings must be arranged, finances planned, publicity drafted, timetables organized. Friends ask how they can help and he doesn't know. Public relations firms offer publicity material. Someone asks where the committee rooms will be. The news media want a biography and photographs.

Sometimes party organizers arrange some of these things for the candidate. Sometimes they don't. When Pauline Jewett first ran for the Liberals in Northumberland in 1962, the party engaged an official photographer. Although there had been opposition to a woman running, she was delighted to receive a personal letter from a high party official. He was glad she had won the nomination, and would do everything he could to help. An appointment had already been made to have her photograph taken. "I would suggest," he wrote, "that you wear a shirt with double cuffs and a dark tie; and appear freshly shaven."

A well-organized candidate realizes he must establish priorities. And the one thing he must do is to file nomination papers. If he does nothing else, his name will still appear on the ballot. But failure means he is not a candidate, and his party is not represented. Candidates are hounded by their party headquarters to get their papers filed early. Five or six weeks of preparation and a lot of money goes down the drain if he is late. He is faced with an embarrassed party and the probability that he will never again be entrusted with anything. But some forget.

Second priority is to plan the door-to-door canvass. Everything else is subordinate. I found it essential to decide at the very beginning where I would work, day by day, throughout the campaign. In large rural constituencies particularly, failure to plan will find the candidate working in one end of his riding, and some event taking place in the other. Time spent travelling is not only wasted, it is exhausting. A half hour rest can leave a candidate fresh and in good humour. Rushing to an event can result in disaster. It happened once to my three-time opponent, Gerald Taylor, who put on a vigorous campaign each time. Rushing to the television station in Barrie, over 100 miles from his home, he came across one of my workers, Bunny Carter, re-arranging road posters.

"What do you think you're doing?" Taylor demanded.

"You have so many signs stuck up all over the place, I couldn't find anywhere to put ours," replied Carter, "so I am just tacking a few over top of yours."

"That's all you're doing, is it?" said Taylor. "Well, I could have you arrested."

"Just try it," said Carter.

But it was late, and Gerald was broadcasting live. So he drove off, becoming more and more furious as he went. Arriving in the studio seconds before his deadline, he missed his starting cue, and appeared stunned when told he was on. Fumbling for his text, he went into a childish tirade about the opposition interfering with his road signs. The effect on television viewers was disastrous. This sort of thing often happens to candidates running late and under pressure.

A candidate with serious intentions of winning will have 300 to 500 people employed, to help him spend between $10,000 and $25,000 in a few short weeks. He needs a campaign manager, a publicity director and a financial agent at the absolute minimum. Although some candidates struggle along with a couple of friends, and win, and others have gigantic organizations and lose, a compact, well-supervised election group can do wonders.

Having disposed of the preliminaries, the candidate can go about his main task of meeting the people. That is best accomplished by presenting himself, door to door, throughout his riding. The object of such a canvass is to meet as many voters as possible and to leave a good impression.

Calling unexpectedly on supposedly private homes can take people at a disadvantage. That is one of the dangers of wholesale door knocking, and the candidate must go prepared. One of the most hilarious and delightful days I ever had canvassing was at the Shawanga Indian Reserve, in company with Irene Pawis, who was for some time Chief, Flora Tabobandung, Chief of the neighbouring Parry Island band and Kay Larmondin, a well-respected local lady. These girls knew everyone on the reserve, their habits, their comings and goings and their friends. We started out in good time in the morning. At one house, they knocked on the door until the place shook, peered in the windows and raised a clamour.

"Come on, get up. We know you're in there," they called out. I would have left, but they hung on.

"No. No. He sleeps like a log. But he wants to see you and he would be really annoyed if we didn't get him up." Sure enough, in about five minutes the door opened, and a soggy unshaven man, in his long underwear, made his appearance.

"We brought Mr. Aiken to see you."

"Who?"

"The Member of Parliament. You wanted to see him."

Recognition finally came, and we were invited in. Nobody else would have gotten away with it.

House by house we progressed through Shawanaga village, disturbing people, visiting, gossiping and incidentally accumulating a nice majority for the coming election. But no candidate could have survived the hazards alone. There is a difference of opinion whether a candidate should be accompanied by a local person when canvassing. Generally, I prefer to go alone. But not always.

On the average Canadian ridings contain 85,000 people. So don't be surprised if you never see a candidate. It is a physical impossibility. But when working an area, the candidate must knock on every door. If going down one side of a city street, he must do the block. On a country road or in a subdivision, he must call at every house. He cannot skip. It is faulty thinking to by-pass a house on the ground that no candidate can visit everyone. A stranger attracts the attention of children, who run and tell their mother. She may have noticed him already. She mentally prepares to greet him, one way or another. He calls next door, then walks right past. She wonders why. Eventually she will come up with an answer, and it will not be complimentary. In some way he has insulted her. If the candidate does not get into the area at all, everyone is treated equally. During one election Harold Danforth was making calls in a community, and began to notice how warmly he was being received. Almost every other person asked him in and praised his efforts to meet the people. Shortly he learned the reason. "That other fellow, what's-his-name, was around here yesterday, but I never saw him," complained one lady, "I was one of his supporters, too. But if my vote isn't worth a call, then he won't get it."

To save time, the other candidate had knocked on alternate doors, and annoyed alternate householders.

Occasionally the candidate's time is purposely wasted by an opposition supporter. He talks and talks, enjoying every passing minute. Of course, abruptness makes no friends either. The mark of an experienced canvasser is to make each call brief and pleasant. Sometimes, without losing pace, a lasting friendship can result from a cup of coffee in someone's kitchen or lunch with the family.

Without being to crude about it, a candidate should request his listener's support or vote. I once talked to an old timer at South River fall fair. I thought I had made a good impression. But later he said to a friend, "I talked to that fellow for ten minutes and he never asked for my vote. I guess he doesn't want it."

You learn to guard against foolish optimism while canvassing door to door. Very few votes are changed in the course of a day. Most people want to be pleasant. They are in their own homes, and they will not be rude to a visitor. But a kind word doesn't mean a vote. In fact, many people spend the entire visit trying to think of something nice to say, without being dishonest. "It was nice of you to call" — "I'll be thinking of you on election day" (how?) — or even, "good luck," often means nothing. I once marked "supporter" opposite the name of a person who told me, "My father was campaign manager for your party for 30 years back home, and the family has always voted that way." But I found out later that he was the free-thinker in the family, and always voted some other way.

A very small percentage of people visited change their vote. The effort resembles a loaded tanker ship at cruising speed, which needs miles to change direction. Constant application of rudder and engines start a movement which eventually becomes noticeable. Canvassing is like that. Vote by vote, house by house, day by day results are achieved. A vote changed counts two, one more for us, one less for them. One changed vote in each poll can mean 300 in total. So it goes, counting votes like drops into a sap bucket. The opposition is working, too. How much more is one candidate achieving than the other? And all those efforts can be blown away like leaves in a windstorm by a change in public sentiment or a decline in the leader's popularity. But the work must go on until the very end.

Every election has its "How did they do it?" stories, and 1972 was no exception. Jim Gillies beat Robert Kaplan in Don Valley, Toronto. Gillies had waged a campaign on all fronts. The day the election was called, he had posters out on the street. On election day, he was still working, with a new idea. On apartment doors throughout the riding doorhangers appeared reading, "Good morning. It's election day. Don't forget to vote. Jim Gillies." During the campaign he knocked on 12,000 doors, wearing out his "victory shoes." It was not canvassing alone that won, but it played a major part. "I think they were just overwhelmed by Jim Gillies," summed up his disappointed opponent.

In Kingston and the Islands, Flora MacDonald surprised a lot

26

of people by winning with nearly 9000 majority. Everyone had been nice, but not that many thought she would actually win. Nevertheless, she was working effectively. "I did a lot of door knocking," she told me, "and I would like to have done a lot more. But I think special events had the most impact, both on them and on me. With well-organized coffee parties, meeting people at work and things like that, you can react with a lot of people." When she was calling at homes near the end of the campaign, people recognized her and called her by name. Then she knew that the tide was turning.

John Harney was making his fifth try for a parliamentary seat. It was crucial for him because he has aspirations for leadership of the New Democratic Party. David Weatherhead was a tough man to beat in Scarborough West. But Harney won. Weatherhead attributes his loss to a strong showing by Conservative Basil Clark. Harney credits door-to-door canvassing. Party workers did six canvasses, a specialty with the New Democrats. Harney does admit to some doubts. "I canvassed full-time in the other elections and lost," he told me. "This time I was out of action for three weeks from illness and won. There must be a message there somewhere."

In Toronto St. Paul's an upset victory by Conservative Ron Atkey over well-established Ian Wahn was attributed to 15,000 personal calls by the candidate, and total coverage of the riding by party workers. There was another person wearing out shoe leather, too. Ron's attractive wife Brenda hardly missed a day.

But Heward Grafftey's win in Brome-Missisquoi is surely proof that personal calls win the victory. He ran against a well-regarded sitting Member, Yves Forest, who had defeated him once before. The tide was against his Progressive Conservative party in Quebec, for only 2 Members were elected out of 74 seats. But Heward had been visiting in the riding while Yves was in Ottawa. During the campaign he canvassed daily, door-to-door, morning to night. He won by 3390 majority.

Believing that the result of personal contact can be measured, I set out to prove it in 1957. The result was the "Magnetawan experiment." Only a few knew it was being conducted. Magnetawan is a quiet little village of about 150 voters. The people have no particular racial, religious or historical bias which would influence their votes. They are friendly, intelligent rural people.

The population is fairly constant. And they voted consistently Liberal from 1926 to 1953. The plan was to put on a concentrated canvass in Magnetawan. I stayed in the village for three days, called at every house and sat down to chat when invited. Evenings were spent at any social event going. By the end of the third day, everyone in the village knew me. And election day, 1957 saw the tide turn. I won.

The picture did not change in ensuing years, because acquaintances made in 1957 grew into friendships, and new residents fell into the pattern. Here is a little table showing 1957 returns and the two elections before and after.

Year	Liberal	Conservative	CCF-NDP
1949	73	40	14
1953	76	38	2
1957	54	65	-
1958	34	73	8
1962	46	68	2

An effort like this doesn't always work. I tried it later in Britt, where voting is rigid, and lost 5 votes. But the odds are worth the effort.

Meeting the people is not often a drag. Most are cordial, and only a few are nasty. Some are especially pleasant. I remember one call at a new and tidy farm house on a country road. When the door opened, there stood a charming young woman, smiling and pretty. A mutual attraction immediately developed. "Come in," she said, "I'm alone, and would just love to talk to someone." All the planned calls at unknown houses suddenly didn't matter. The rule about calls-per-hour and the projected area coverage went down the drain. I went in.

Sitting comfortably in a pleasant living room, the world outside disappeared. We were two people who liked each other. We talked about everything, people, ideas, loneliness. Unconsciously the conversation turned inward, and we were talking about ourselves. Then a long pause, a slight blush, revealed the same thought. If we liked each other so well, should we do something about it? "I often imagine this situation when I am driving," I confessed "finding a lovely girl like you, alone at home and. . . friendly. But it hasn't happened before." "I imagine it too," she said, "the interesting stranger arriving at my door. Someone I know about. Someone who finds me attractive. I'm very excited."

Our eyes met with complete understanding. We visualized the embrace, the pleasure, the separation, with throbbing satisfaction. There was a magic moment that would never pass. Then the restraints of civilization overcame that strong primitive longing. She settled back ever so slightly in her chair, and we basked in the warm glow of companionship. Eventually I knew I had to go. "I really would like to stay longer," I said, "but that might be dangerous." "I know," she replied, "but it has been wonderful having this time together. I feel I have known you for years." As we reached the door, she held up her face and I kissed her gently. It was one of the better days.

The average political meeting these days is a dead loss. The only people who go are the loyal party supporters and they spend their time patting each other on the back, drinking tea and coffee (or hard stuff if provided) and eating sandwiches and cake. The organizers rent too big a hall, and the caretaker sets out every chair he can find. To offset the danger that the press might report a half-empty hall, other organizers bring in bus loads of supporters from far and wide to fill the chairs.

About seven minutes after the meeting starts, the public address system goes dead, and the guest speaker has to shout his way through his notes. One advantage is that he cuts it short. It is not lack of preparation or poor equipment. Pierre Trudeau, as Prime Minister, found himself making signs to his audience when the sound failed in Toronto in 1968. The same thing happened at a heavyweight Conservative meeting in Barrie in October 1972. National leader Stanfield, Premier William Davis of Ontario and numerous candidates had to shout out their abbreviated messages, until adjustments were made. There is something perverse about PA systems.

But meetings are still held, nevertheless. They provide some sort of camaraderie for discouraged workers, and keep them going till the campaign is over. Much more successful from the voter aspect are small coffee parties held in private homes. Friendly neighbours drop in to meet the candidate and have a cup of tea. Generally ladies appear, but now and then one lone gentleman shows up.

After knocking on doors one by one, or meeting a few people in small groups, a candidate almost goes off his rocker when he finds a crowd of people, gathered together by someone else. Here are hands to grasp, and votes to influence. And if he could just get on that platform and charm them with a little speech, he would get them all at once. It is little wonder that candidates show up at almost any event. I used to wonder why politicians were always at these affairs. Why couldn't the "mother of the year" crown the beauty queen, or the oldest man open the fair? The town bum could open the new post office — he will monopolize the steps. Well, it's because politicians are willing. They don't have to be coaxed. Just offer them a platform or a crowd, and they will appear. Eventually they get invited to everything, and can't keep up with it.

"We have brought it on ourselves," said P.B. "Doc" Rynard when we discussed the many invitations Members get. "A politician does it for exposure. Anyone else exposing himself would be arrested."

Another method of being seen and heard at election time is through radio and television. The mass exposure to voters the candidate cannot reach is very appealing. In many areas, a few broadcasts are imperative. Sometimes to spice it up a bit, candidates bring in a guest to interview them; or even have someone else speak on their behalf.

Doug Fisher, newsman and former Member, once went to Timmins to help out Murdo Martin in his election campaign. Doug did a live television program in which he was using flip charts to illustrate his point. When the time came for the camera to move in on the charts, nothing happened. Furtively looking around to see what was wrong, Doug kept right on talking, like the pro he is. Finally he saw the cameraman standing off to one side of the studio, joking with Murdo Martin, whom Doug was supposed to be helping.

Sometimes the fumbles turn out right. In the 1968 election, Craig Stewart became a candidate in Marquette, Manitoba after the election was called. He had neither time nor experience, but plunged ahead with his campaign. An opponent advertised giant bean-and-wiener parties on the Indian reserves the Sunday before voting day. On television, Craig was asked if he planned anything like that. He said not.

"Then what effect do you think these bean parties will have?" persisted the interviewer. Craig was tired, and without too much thought he answered flippantly, "Well, they sound like a lot of hot air to me."

Afterwards he was told the remark was crude, and would do a lot of harm. However, a lot of people thought the answer very funny. They made jokes about it right at the bean parties.On election day, Craig won the Indian reserves — and the election.

Election time is fiasco time. About 1,000 candidates for election are doing their best, in one way or another, to impress their constituents with their fine qualities and their suitability to be the Member of Parliament. Each of these candidates has anywhere from 15 to 50 enthusiastic local organizers going about the job in their own way. Some of their ideas are crafty, bordering on the dishonest. Some fairly common practices shock new candidates, but they go along if it means winning. So the most amazing things happen. A candidate and his manager can spend as much time smoothing out messes as in positive campaign work. Losers look back on these messes with pangs of regret; winners can afford to laugh about them. A group of winners was sitting around the lobby of the House of Commons waiting for a vote one night, when someone started on the subject. "I don't know why they do it," said one. "This little community couldn't turn out 50 people to watch the Leafs play the Bruins in the local arena. But they packed 150 chairs into the hall for my meeting. With a record turn-out of 35, the place looked empty."

"That's nothing to what they did to me," responded another. "The committee decided on a garden party. Everything was set up perfectly: beautiful grounds, food, beverages and music. They hadn't overlooked anything — except the invitations. About six of us sat around all afternoon, waiting for somebody else to turn up. I figure it cost about $50.00 a person."

Quarrelling workers, enthusiastic bunglers, illegal dispensers of liquor, and people with bright ideas that backfire are among the dozens of misdirected efforts of any campaign. The people who dreamed up the idea of bugging opposition headquarters in 1972 didn't do President Richard Nixon much good, either. But that all turned up after it was over. The candidate himself is no exception. He goes around fouling up carefully laid local plans. He arrives late for meetings and events. He makes off-hand statements, or ignorant ones, which make the whole effort look foolish. He fails to clamp down on workers who finally get the campaign into trouble.

As well-ordered enterprises, most campaigns are disasters.

And as a final word, a candidate should know his opponent. In 1963, the fall fair at Rosseau was held just a few days before the Ontario provincial election. As Rosseau borders two provincial ridings, the place was overrun with candidates. Dorothy Sleeth, a candidate in Parry Sound riding engaged a responsible-looking man in friendly conversation. She concluded by asking him to vote for her.

"I would just love to, dear," said Allie Johnston, the gallant sitting Member, "but I am running myself."

Suddenly, one Saturday night, the campaign is over. Nothing is left but to bring in the vote. You sit at home, wondering if it was all a bad dream. How much integrity has been sacrificed to gain votes and to keep things running smoothly? Was it worth the effort? For the new candidate who becomes Member, it's the first of many times he will ask himself the same questions.

THE WINNER

"Every Vote Counts"

Clustered in small groups, the opponents in the judge's chamber shuffled uneasily as they awaited the decision. Throughout the entire proceeding, it had been obvious that the result would be close, and now the moment of truth was approaching. The judge sat vacantly staring into space; this time the decision was not his. Out on the chilly street another man walked, and on him the burden lay.

Returning Officer J. Denzil Moodie had been through a lot in the last two months. The welter of details in organizing enumeration of the voters, printing of lists, getting out the ballot boxes and finally supervising the vote in a few short weeks had been exhausting. Election night April 8th, 1963 had left the two main contenders only a few votes apart. The unusual procedure of a judicial recount had dragged out his duties. And now this incredible thing had happened. Sitting Member Paul Martineau and Liberal challenger Paul Goulet had come out of the recount with exactly six thousand, four hundred and forty-eight votes each. There was no room for argument. Each lawyer had wrung out every last vote for his client; the judge had ruled on every doubtful ballot. The totals were checked and rechecked, but it always came out the same — a tie vote. And the law now required the Returning Officer to decide who would be the Member of Parliament for Pontiac-Temiscamingue. As he walked, he recalled thinking vaguely that this might happen. But now, the decision was upon him. Then it came to him what he must do. He turned back toward the court room.

After Moodie had asked for a few minutes to consider his problem alone, the others sat thinking about that one vote. One extra call by the candidate during the campaign; one more voter rooted out on election day could have made the difference. So many had been overlooked in the mad rush of the election campaign. It would have been possible then to do something — it was impossible now.

The sound of the door opening brought everyone back to the present. The Returning Officer approached the judge and announced his decision. Since the sitting Member had not been defeated, he cast his vote for Martineau. Adding one more digit to the last column, the judge signed the official return. Paul Martineau was elected. There was nothing more to be done. Everyone got up and left quietly.

It does not happen like that often. But every close vote leaves candidates and worker wondering why they did not make that little extra effort. Every vote counts. In a close fight, one or two votes elects a Member. That Member could give his party the seat necessary to elect a government, or defeat one. That is the light in which experienced candidates and workers approach election day. As the returns rolled in on election night, 1972, with Liberals leading by one seat, then Conservatives by one, then parties tied 108-108, workers in close ridings, and those who did not work, reflected on tasks undone. A little more effort could have changed the result. Not only that year, either. In the minority situations of 1957, 1962, 1963 and 1965, a small number of votes in a few ridings would have changed the course of history.

There are no sure seats. On October 21, 1972 an article in the Toronto Star described Liberal Ian Wahn as a "shoo-in" in St. Paul's. Ten days later he was defeated. It is unlikely that an experienced Member like Wahn was unconcerned, but no doubt some of his workers were. In the language of 1882, oft repeated to this day, Sir John A. Macdonald soliloquized, "An election is like a horse-race in that you can tell more about it the next day." And another less famous Canadian, Joseph-Israel Tarte added an appropriate postscript in 1896: "Elections are not won by prayers alone." Tarte obviously knew. His first election to the House of Commons in April 1891, for Montmorency, was declared void for irregularities. And after that he hung in by changing ridings four times, and changing parties twice. Oddly enough, he ended up in the cabinet.

On election day, the objective is favourable votes in the ballot box. Nothing else. Howard Green, then Secretary of State for External Affairs was defeated in Vancouver-Quadra in the 1963 election. It was a stunning defeat for a man who had been elected continuously for that riding since 1935. Reporters were curious as to the reason. Some said that as cabinet minister, Green had been away from the riding too much. Some claimed that Mr. Diefenbaker's popularity had dropped so far that Green was dragged down with it. Some wondered whether his handling of External Affairs had any effect.

"Mr. Green," asked a reporter directly, "to what do you attribute your defeat in Vancouver-Quadra?"

A slight smile appeared on Howard Green's face. He was well known for his straightforward comments, and reporters grasped their pencils firmly, ready to get it all down.

"The real reason is," he pronounced, "I didn't get enough votes."

Workers show up for their duties on election day with opinion polls, forecasts and predictions ringing in their ears. The professional polls are the ones taken most seriously and in Canada that means the Gallup poll. It is conducted by the Canadian Institute of Public Opinion which bases its report on interviews with 700 of some 22,000,000 Canadians. That is a very small percentage, but the operators claim it is enough. They publish the results but do not predict the outcome. Interpretation of the result is left to the individual, and that's where the amateurs are in trouble.

Polls have a noticeable effect on workers. If the party and leader are away ahead, and there is little movement from the last poll, the result can be complacency. A good many "safe" Liberals and their workers interpreted the polls as satisfactory in 1972 and later found themselves defeated. There are two real dangers. A national or provincial average has little relevance to an individual riding and a last minute movement of undecided voters can not be forecast.

On the other hand, an adverse poll is hard on candidates and workers. It seems to say, "Work all you like, it won't do any good." Experienced workers know that a poll is something to quote, if favourable — and to ignore, if unfavourable. Professional polls taken in their true perspective can be useful. But they have been away off. In 1957, they indicated a win in Canada for Louis St. Laurent. In 1970 they indicated a win in Britain for Harold Wilson. They were wrong both times. So the moral is, just keep on working.

Some people see dangers to the democratic process in the publication of pre-election polls. They fear a band-wagon effect, a rush of voters to the winning side. That's not the way it appears. Favourable polls did not save St. Laurent in 1957 or Wilson in 1970. They probably kept the opposition working desperately for every last vote. The man who should know is Dr. George Gallup, founder of the Gallup poll. He was recently quoted as saying: "The politicians are absolutely convinced that if they can only show they're running well, that's going to put them over. This is the biggest myth in the business, but I suppose it buoys their spirits and the people around them. It's absolutely nutty."

Then there are the private professional polls. They are not only unpublished, they are secretly guarded. Trudeau apparently decided against a summer election in 1972 because of an adverse poll taken by professionals. The poll was probably correct. The only thing it did not do was forecast the future, which was worse. The Stanfield team under national organizer Finley Macdonald and national director Liam O'Brian had a fair idea of the future trend from their own polls, and adapted to it.

Now we come to the pundits. Mostly, they are members of the parliamentary press gallery. This is the group of observant, intelligent reporters who spend 365 days each year living with politics and politicians. To maintain professional standing,they must periodically undergo the ordeal of election forecasting. Some approach it eagerly, like a moth attracted to an open flame. Others are concerned about their integrity, and approach it cautiously. Other people can hedge their words on election night, but not the writers. They are indelibly in print, and their mistakes exposed. The most famous unprotected and mistaken forecast was made by Blair Fraser in 1957. He wrote in MacLean's magazine that the Liberals had won, but his forecast, printed in advance as fact, was badly out. He took the sting of that one to his untimely death.

Charles Lynch also had his share of woe. Let him tell it himself, from his column published on November 1st, 1972: "Am eating crow from beneath a load of raspberries for having predicted the Liberals would win big." Lynch was particularly humiliated because, as with previous bloopers, he was writing from experience on the campaign trail. George Brimmell, an executive editor who never left the office, called it right.

Douglas Fisher, a former Member with four election wins to his credit, changed his luck with his profession. "The federal Liberals have reason to coast along at their present campaign pace," he wrote during the 1972 campaign, quoting opinion polls as his source. They were wrong.

Farmer Tissington of the Thompson newspapers tried the bellwether approach. Scientifically examining returns in Prince Edward Island for the past ten elections, he concluded a few days before the election: "Return of one or more Liberals in P.E.I. could be the forerunner of a Liberal victory greater than 1968." His conclusion was wrong. The Liberals did return one Member from P.E.I. But they crashed nationally.

If the professional forecasters can't tell, then who can?

At 8:00 o'clock in the morning, standard time on election day the polls open. At each of 61,000 polling stations across Canada the deputy returning officer places the ballot box on the table, arranges the ballot papers and instruction books and sits down to start work. Beside her (for most are women) sits the poll clerk, with a copy of the voters list and a poll book in which to record the names of those who have voted. Located beside these officials are the agents of the candidates, the scrutineers, whose main job is to keep a similar list.

The first customer is generally waiting for the deputy to finish swearing everyone to secrecy. He receives his ballot, takes it to a private booth nearby and marks it. He then returns it to the deputy, who checks her initials on the counterfoil which she then removes, and the ballot goes into the box. The democratic process is under way. It will be a long day for everyone. The voting continues throughout the day without break for lunch or dinner until the polls close at 7:00 p.m. After that, it will take anything from 10 to 90 minutes to count the vote and report.

As the day begins at the nearby party nerve centres, drivers show up with cars ready to start work. Poll supervisor and driver sit down to map out the timetable. There are already requests for rides to the poll at specified times. There is always some confusion as things start to go wrong. Someone does not report for duty. Someone else arrives, and does not know what to do. Two people are doing the same job. One of the scrutineers forgot to take lunch. But the well-managed office shortly settles down to an effective hum, as it prepares to get every favourable voter to the poll.

Shortly the first list of those who have voted comes in from the scrutineer. The names are stroked off from a marked list. This list is the key to the operation. A good canvass has identified any indication of voting intentions. The canvassers and a group of local supporters have already gone over the list, and the favourable, unfavourable and doubtful voters are indicated. On some names there was disagreement. The canvasser was well received, and given words of encouragement. But a neighbour has never known that person to favour the party. Does it mean a changed vote this election, or was the canvasser misled? A decision has been made, and the name marked with a code letter. Today,when every supporter has voted, the job will be done. If there is time, those marked "possible" can be brought in. But then they stop. A political organization does not exist to bring in votes for a poorly-run opposition. Public service and good deeds will be provided by the candidate when he is elected.

Emergencies arise in every committee room. Sometimes they are created by the opposition. One little trick to prepare for is the telephone spoiler. At the busiest time of the day, between 5:00 and 7:00 p.m. someone calls the committee room from a pay phone, then walks off without hanging up. In most systems, the telephone is then out of service. To prevent disaster, most committee rooms have one unlisted.

Back at the polling station the scrutineer generally has it easy these days. Federal election procedures are designed to eliminate foul play. But occasionally shades of the past revive, and the scrutineer must do the job for which he was named. Scrutinizing the vote implies the reporting of illegal activities and prevention of unauthorized votes.

Physical violence occurs very seldom in Canada on polling day, but when it does the object is either to cover up illegal activities or to discourage certain people from voting. The government in power technically has the means of controlling election activities through the appointments it makes. So if some zealous poll officials want to stuff ballot boxes or falsify records, strong-arm characters keep people out of the poll while it is happening. Also in a strongly anti-government area, people can be frightened away from the polls by the occurrence of violence.

More common is the practise of impersonation. This allows some people to get several votes. In its worst form, a group of people go from poll to poll in a riding, casting votes in the names of persons who are not likely to show up. There are plenty of refinements of that system. Sometimes the names of people who are not entitled to vote because of citizenship, age, or residence appear on the voters list. Some try to vote anyway. Challenging such people is the scrutineer's real job, but it is not encouraged by most candidates, because it can cost votes. "I guess we lost those two," said my agent ruefully, after unsuccessfully challenging a couple he didn't recognize, causing an angry scene at the polling booth.

Great precautions are taken to maintain secrecy. Many people would not vote if they thought anyone knew how they voted. They may have connections of some sort with the government. They may decide for once in their life to vote against their party. And secrecy is almost 100 per cent successful. But there are loopholes and accidents. One deputy returning officer who had been at the job for years, had a neighbour who talked out of both sides of his mouth. He supported everybody. He could always say afterwards that he supported the winning candidate, the successful party. He was not only a hypocrite but a tiresome one. So the DRO devised a little method of marking one ballot; and when that ballot came out of the box on election night, he knew.

"I never told anybody for a long time," he confessed to me, "but one night I got fed up with that fellow, and I told him. I figured he wouldn't be any more anxious for the story to get out than I was. He never talked politics in my presence again."

Sometimes everyone knows how a person voted. It happens when only one vote is cast in a poll; or when all the votes are the same way. More than one deputy returning officer in a remote area has opened the poll, cast his own ballot, then waited all day in vain for someone else to appear. At closing time, he has had to count his own vote and report it. That polling division is usually closed before the next election. It is especially embarrassing for election officials appointed by one party to be found voting for another.

Funny work at the polls sometimes results in a new election. Erik Nielsen was first elected for the Yukon in 1957 when his opponent's win was voided for breaches of the Election Act. Richard Cashin had his 1962 election in St. John's West declared invalid, and had to leave Ottawa until he won the general election in April 1963. Rom Barnett lost Burnaby-Coquitlam by 9 votes in 1968, but after it was set aside, he won the by-election. And following the tie vote in Pontiac-Temiscamingue in 1963, court proceedings were brought by Goulet over irregularities. But every time Goulet proved some improper practices by Martineau's workers, Martineau proved just as many the other way. It was an impasse. The proceedings dragged wearily on during the entire 25th parliament, and had not been concluded when the 1965 election was called.

Money is a problem for everyone at election time. Past scandals make people sensitive, and January 1974 saw tighter controls imposed on Federal election spending. Businesses nowadays donate to two or more parties, just to be safe. No matter what is done, the candidate generally gets caught between what he spends and what is collected for him. For some, it takes two or three years to recover. Right now, candidates in the two major parties declare an average of $15,000 for election expenses. Twenty years ago it was $4500.

Election day, however, is not the time to worry about expense. There is more value for the dollar in getting people out to the polls than in anything else. The new proxy voting system in Canada required a lot of running around for every vote. But in some ridings, cars were rounded up and proxy voters were taken to the polls on election day. It meant sure votes each trip. Transportation managers often get requests to send a car 15 or 20 miles to pick up a voter. If it's a sure vote, there is no hesitation. The only question is whether someone in the opposition is fouling up your transportation system.

Although money can help win an election, it can no longer buy an election in the crude sense. Those who go through the experience know that if you are a loser, no amount of money can save you. The best proof in modern times was the 1957 election. Giant after Liberal giant went down to defeat spending $75,000 or $100,000, soundly beaten by upstarts with a couple of thousand dollars and a lot of willing workers. But the practice of throwing around money at election time still continues.

Pauline Jewett had her eyes opened the first time she ran. She had a poll captain who was skeptical about a woman running in a rural riding. However, if she gave him the money, he promised to deliver the poll. When he mentioned $300 she gasped, for it was a very small poll. But he said that everyone had some special need, something around the house, some entertainment. It would all be looked after. When she asked how he could be sure of their vote in the secrecy of the polling booth, he replied angrily: "Miss Jewett, these are honest people." It wasn't much different a hundred years ago. Edward Blake revealed for posterity how they made sure in the days of hard-line party voting. "If you buy a man to stay at home," he commented in a speech at Aurora, Ontario, "you can always tell whether he has kept his bargain or not."

Election day weather strategists always seem to have divergent views. "Let's hope for a bright day," someone supporting the government says. "It will make people feel better and things won't look so bad after all." "We will be better off with rain," says another. "Only the committed party voters will turn out, and this riding leans to the government party." On Sunday evening, October 29th, 1972 radio and television audiences heard the usual pre-election forecasts. "Liberal strategists are hoping for good weather and a large turn-out for voting tomorrow," read the announcer. The reasoning was not explained, but presumably strategists somewhere thought the big uncommitted vote was just waiting for a nice day. They were wrong. The day came clear and bright across the country, there was a big turn-out and things went bad for the Liberals.

In fact, a large turn-out bodes no good for government supporters. People turn out to express their dissatisfaction, not their appreciation. The best place to look for an example is probably the Ottawa area in 1972. Here are the four ridings in the capital area with the highest voter presence. The results speak for themselves. The government supporter who wants a big turn-out must have holes in his head.

Turnout	Riding	Result for the Government
83%	Ottawa West	Defeat of Member
81%	Leeds	Defeat of candidate
80%	Frontenac-Lennox and Addington	Defeat of candidate
80%	Lanark-Renfrew-Carleton	Defeat of Member

In 8 other ridings, with turnout from 78 percent to 60 percent, only one government Member or candidate was defeated.

Ontario voters should have guessed how things would go. In judging the accuracy of the Globe and Mail's switch to the Liberals, they could compare its other predictions for the day. On that bright, clear election morning the front page headline read:

CLOUDY, COLD WEATHER GREETS VOTERS TODAY

When the polls close at 7:00 p.m., there is a lull in committee rooms and poll headquarters. The job is done, for better or worse. Now they can only wait for the results to come in. It is a different story in the polling stations. The deputy returning officer, poll clerk and scrutineers begin to find out how all those votes have been cast. One by one, the ballot papers are taken out of the box and counted. Sometimes those at the top tell a story. If they are mostly for one candidate, it means his workers have pushed out their last minute voters. Each scrutineer feels responsible for his own candidate. Excitement builds up as the result takes shape. It may be a landslide. Or it may see-saw back and forth among two or three candidates until the last vote is tallied.

In some rural polls, the captain has every vote counted before it is cast. There are only a few electors likely to change in these polls, and during one difficult election, a poll captain said to me: "You know, I think that rascal up the concession is going to jump the fence and vote against us. He and his wife always split their votes, but this time she has him wavering."

"Would it do any good if I went to see them?" I asked.

"Well, it wouldn't do any harm," said Mervin Hall, "they say you have never called on them."

So I went and had a pleasant half hour with a very nice couple. There were several things bothering them and we talked it out. They didn't say much when I left except, "I suppose Merv. Hall sent you down to see us."

"That's right. He was worried about some things you said."

"Well," replied the husband, "we'll think it over."

On election day, driver Hall picked up both husband and wife and took them to vote. After the election was over, he had something to tell me.

"Say, you know that couple I sent you down to see? I think maybe you got both votes, because I was one up on my count election night."

They can have it figured that close.

As reports come into committee rooms and the returning office on election night, a crowd gathers and returns are cheered or lamented. Someone always wins. There are times when observers feel that nobody deserves to win. One candidate has done nothing, and the others have followed suit. Sometimes the candidate who seemed best suited for the job is defeated. The one who did everything wrong is elected. These things can be rationalized. Parliament would be a shambles with 264 supermen. All the same, it leaves some candidates and their workers sick with the inconsistency of the public while others are delighted with it.

Five votes gave the Liberals the most seats in 1972. On November 15th, the outcome was a tie; 108 seats for the Liberals, 108 seats for the Progressive Conservatives. Recounts had been held in all doubtful ridings but one.

In Oshawa, Ontario, on that November day, Judge Joseph Kelly was conducting a judicial recount of the ballots cast in the riding of Ontario. The election-night return had given Conservative Frank McGee a majority of 12 over Liberal incumbent Norman Cafik. At 11:20 p.m. the judge declared the result in writing.

Cafik had won by 4 votes, with 16,324. Five people somewhere in Ontario county riding who got to the polls to vote for Cafik, not only elected him Member, but gave Pierre Trudeau a two-seat majority instead of a tie. These are times when a vote matters a lot. About 10,000,000 Canadians voted in the 1972 elections. Five decided who won. As with the Martineau tie, these razor-sharp decisions only happen occasionally. But there are always close ones, and there is no way of knowing in advance when or where they will come. By an accident of fate, Robert Stanfield's candidate lost in all three 1972 recounts. Fifty more votes in the right place would have given him three more ridings and the most seats in Parliament.

Members who have seen these close decisions, in the constituency and nationally, are very conscious of the value of a vote. A constituent offended may mean a vote lost. A community neglected may mean 25 lost. Someone helped may mean a vote won. A group pleased may mean 25 won. He knows that keeping up the big smile, the glad hand and the constituency work may just let him squeak in again next time. It doesn't encourage unpopular activites.

Back to Toronto for an object lesson along these lines. Liberal Steve Otto was defeated in York East, a seat he had held for 10 years. Steve was an independent sort of Member. He often spoke out against government actions and came close to being a rebel. But when the chips were down in 1972, he relented. "I backed Trudeau all the way and it cost me my seat," said Steve after the election.

Perry Ryan was a ten-year Liberal Member and rebel too. But he handled it the other way. He left the party and joined the Progressive Conservatives. He was also defeated. "Mr. Stollery has demonstrated his claim that the party runs ahead of the man," Perry told a quiet committee room in Spadina after his loss to Liberal Peter Stollery was confirmed.

Who then was neighbour to these two men who made up their minds firmly and fell among voters? Which of them did the right thing? Neither, according to their constituents. They should both have kept their mouths shut, and coasted along quietly. Then maybe they would have been re-elected. That's the way it is.

THE LEARNER

"I'm New At This Game"

The chill of approaching winter was once more in the air when I arrived in Ottawa to stay. Yellow leaves still clung forlornly to the trees as the autumn winds tugged away at them fitfully. Occasional shafts of sunlight were quickly obscured by dark clouds. But inside the grey stone walls of parliament's Centre Block, the mood was excited and alive. The crystalline arches in the main entrance shone brightly in the glow of television lights as they funnelled down to meet the marble pillars. A sparkle of polished brass reflected from the dress uniforms of the aides-de-camp and the scarlet tunics of the Royal Canadian Mounted Police. The corridors were packed with guests, conversing in hushed voices as the protective staff kept the entrance clear.

It was October 14th, 1957, a year after I had made the decision to run for parliament. Now the opening day of my first session had arrived. Marie and some friends, dressed in their best formal attire, were already seated in the Senate Chamber. At 3:00 p.m. the assembly bells began to ring, and I rushed off towards my new seat in the House of Commons. But as I passed the main entrance I saw several veteran Members standing there casually, as if there was all the time in the world. They told me nothing would happen until after the Governor General arrived, so there was no hurry. The Prime Minister, dressed in a morning coat, was waiting at the main door. New cabinet ministers, some in parliament for the first time, stood around nervously in their long-tailed coats. The commoners, like myself, wore ordinary dark suits.

Outside, the roar of motorcycles suddenly echoed from the walls of the surrounding buildings, and the first gun of the royal salute boomed across the city of Ottawa. Then followed the clap-clap of horses' hooves as the mounted escort and the Governor General himself arrived. After an expectant hush, the main doors swung open and the official party entered. As spectators watched with emotion, the regal procession moved through the echoing halls to the Senate Chamber. Then the Members sauntered off to the Commons to await the return of the Prime Minister from his escort duties.

In that first official opening, the least impressive person was its central figure, Governor General Vincent Massey, a Canadian of great intellect and ability, made little physical impact. Small of stature, slightly stooped, and in modest attire he was outshone by all around him. The message he gave was that greatness can be enshrouded in a common frame. Yet there was something regal in the very presence of his successor, General Georges Vanier. Tall and impressive, his military bearing was accentuated by the slight limp of a wounded veteran. Gov. General Roland Michener was likewise an impressive person, handsome and friendly. A feeling of satisfaction that this man was first in precedence among Canadians always welled up in those who watched him perform his duties. Our new first citizen, Jules Léger, has made an auspicious start.

Taking my seat in the Commons, I was for once happy that my surname starts with an "A". For the 70 new Members were seated alphabetically from the front, and I got a third row seat, rather than a fifth. From this vantage point, I watched Major C.R. Lamoureux, Gentleman Usher from the Senate, deliver his message that the Governor General awaited. Following our newly-elected Speaker, the same Roland Michener who later became Governor General, we all trooped down the halls to the Senate chamber to hear the Speech from the Throne. Shortly returning with our work for the session outlined, we settled down then to make history, in our own special way.

One thing fascinated me about that first opening. Major Lamoureux, a double amputee, had a tough problem. He had to walk the length of the Commons Chamber, make his announcement, bow, turn and retire to the door, stopping twice to turn and bow. For a man with two wooden legs, this was no mean feat. When he finally reached the door, he was given loud applause by the Members. Officially, it's a mark of respect for the Senate messenger. For him, it was acclaim for successfully manoeuvring the obstacle course. On one memorable occasion, a couple of years later, we had another brilliant display of parliamentary leg work. Col. Pierre Sevigny, Associate Minister of Defence, and a war amputeee, accompanied the Prime Minister to greet new Governor General Vanier. From the main door, General Vanier led off the procession with a regal limp, followed heavily by Col. Sevigny, with Major Lamoureux bringing up the rear.

A few days after that first session began, we watched the "parliamentary magician" do his trick. On every recorded vote the Members stand in turn to be counted. Gordon Dubroy, clerk assistant, has the job of naming each Member as he stands. And if there are two Members with similar names, he also calls out the riding for clarity. This is no easy task. In fact, it is doubtful if any Member can name his 263 colleagues on sight even after 4 years. In 1957, Dubroy had 3 sitting days.

Newcomers who are not forewarned watch with amazement. "That fellow will never name me," thinks the new Member in the fifth row at the far end. "He can hardly even see me. And I'm certain we have never met." But as he stands, his name rings out loud and clear.

How is it done? I have seen magicians do acts like this, but they are not tricks. It is straight organization of memory. It's the same with Dubroy. He has no props, no hidden microphone. He can not rhyme off the names in sequence, for he never knows who will be absent. But his effort starts long before the House assembles. During the election campaign, he follows each riding. He watches for names and pictures of Members elected. When the Members arrive names, faces and ridings come together. After a few days of practise, he is ready. Even old-timers continue to be impresssed. In 1958, after Dubroy had correctly named over 100 new Members, veteran Harold Winch got to his feet. "Our congratulations," he said, "for recognizing everybody by name or constituency on the first division." And everyone applauded in agreement.

Gordon Dubroy still performs regularly.

But it's association with national personalities that leaves the greatest impression on newcomers. People you have read about, watched on television and admired or disliked are now your colleagues. Regardless of the prominence a new Member has had in private life, he now feels at the centre of things, shaping the destiny of the country. For a while everything supports this feeling. His most casual comments are reported widely. He is seen on television by friends and supporters. His views are appreciated in caucus. He is mentioned somewhere, by someone, as cabinet material. His association with important people broadens. I remember my first meeting with the Queen and Prince Philip. There was a long reception line, and as we approached the royal couple, I rehearsed something interesting to say. But just before we reached them, a bodyguard stepped over and admonished: "Don't squeeze Her Majesty's hand."

I was taken aback for a moment but recognized the problem. Hearty squeezers can leave your hand feeling like pulp, I recalled, and hundreds of them must be murder. By now I had passed the royal couple with a light handshake, completely forgetting my intelligent remarks.

Visiting Presidents, Prime Ministers, and officials swell the personal as well as the head. Invited to banquets, receptions and important events, the new Member meets and talks with national and world figures in business, sports and government. The world seems to be within his grasp.

Then the truth begins to emerge. I guess the first shock I got was watching the defeated Prime Minister, Louis St. Laurent, in his place as Leader of the Opposition. He sat with his grey head bowed forward, his heavy glasses standing out against his pale face. When occasion required it, he would rise slowly to his feet, make a brief statement and slump back into his seat. When the daily routine was over, he got up and left quietly, with only a polite nod to those nearby. Walking slowly to his office, he hardly noticed the respectful salutes from the protective staff and the whispered recognition of visitors. His world had fallen apart. Attention was now focussed on those who might succeed him. His nine years as Prime Minister were gone, faded away in defeat. It was an object lesson for any private Member whose self-importance was beginning to emerge.

The second truth I soon learned was that speeches are treated as an outflow of words, expanded or contracted to fit the time available. The studies by C. Northcote Parkinson on the organization of time indicate that work expands to fill the time available. In parliament it works either way, depending on party strategy.

Members on the government side generally find their speeches contracted to zero.

"I know you're hot on this subject," says the House Leader, whose job it is to get legislation passed, "but if you speak, half a dozen others will too. We want this bill passed today, and I think the opposition is just about finished."

In the same debate, the opposition may be stalling for time. "How about speaking on this bill?" says the Opposition House Leader. "You were crying to make a speech a few days ago." "Yes, but it was on another subject," says the eager new Member.

"That's all right, try and fit it in some way."

Every Member arrives in Ottawa with a mission. He had probably got into politics on that account. He has talked about it during his campaign. He has pictured himself getting up in parliament within a couple of weeks at least, and really blowing the roof off. But everything runs along as if he were not there. The people on the front benches seem to get the floor, and by the time they are finished the day is over. He is catching on to another truth. His dearly-loved party isn't really interested in his private projects. They have enough on their hands with general public business. The cabinet ministers are fighting among themselves for time to get their own bills passed. The opposition has to establish its position on government proposals. Not only is the Member on his own, there are 263 others fighting for equal time.

Coming from a resort area, my big beef was government neglect of the tourist industry. The third largest producer of foreign revenue, it was the forgotten child of the federal government. I had plenty to propose. So I tried to get on the throne speech debate.

"Sorry," said Bob Fairnie in the whip's office, "there are already about 30 on the list. You'll never make it this time."

"What's the next opportunity?"

"The budget is the next general debate," replied Bob, "I'll put you on that list."

"But that might be months," I protested, "people are already asking me why I haven't spoken."

"You can talk to the Whip if you like," said Bob, "but he generally takes them in order."

So I decided to try something else.

"Why don't you ask a question," someone suggested, "you can't make it too tough on your own minister, so talk to him first."

The Minister wasn't ready for a question.

"We're working on it," he said. "Give us some time. Why don't you put a bill or motion on the order paper."

After a lot of work and expert advice, I found the subject was too broad for one bill. And nobody seemed anxious to help put it into words. Resolutions can be pretty general, I learned, so I drafted one. But other events caught up with me. The House suddenly dissolved. There was no budget debate. I never got to mention my pet project during my first parliament.

This is pretty typical. Members in the opposition are no better off. The rules are designed to let private Members talk, if there is time. Speeches are only words, reported and applauded, but they bring little action.

Bills moved by private Members are allotted one hour for discussion. The government makes sure they do not come to a vote by having the discussion continue till the hour is over. Then they disappear to the bottom of a long list. Resolutions get the same treatment. And even if passed, they are not binding on anyone. They are only good intentions, expressed in writing.

Written questions go unanswered as long as possible; then they bring only what is asked.

Oral questions to ministers get evasive answers, but recent rules allow an unsatisfied Member to discuss his question for seven minutes at the 10:00 p.m. adjournment hour. Still and all, it's only another speech. Nothing results.

Going to the minister from either side of the House is generally fruitless. If your proposal is good, the government may use it some time later, without acknowledgement. Otherwise, they can give you reasons why it won't work.

Bluntly stated, private Members in Canada do not make new laws. Theoretically it is possible. They are encouraged to try. But everything is stacked against them. "The fullest discussion is encouraged on any question raised by private Members," wrote Arthur Beauchesne, Clerk of the House and rules expert, when discussing bills of the private Member in 1933. "But he must command a majority in the House to secure adoption of his own measures."

Since only the Prime Minister commands that majority, the truth is pretty clear. And the situation hasn't changed much since 1933, either. Reading a lot of American periodicals, some Canadians confuse the systems. In the United States, private Members do sponsor general public laws and see them passed. Major bills are often named after the sponsors. But the executive power is not present in Congress, as is the ministry in Canada. With a majority of the Members backing it, the Canadian government makes the laws.

While there is little chance of a private Member's proposal being accepted, the rules and the ministers actually encourage the effort. It's something like an "Opportunities for MP's" program, keeping them busy at thinking up ideas and making speeches.

Some Members, when they finally get wise to the facts, stop wasting their time. All they get out of it is a little item in the news, if their idea is crazy enough. Often they don't even get that. Then when they get through a second election, and find it didn't make any difference anyway, they give up on private law-making. Others cheerfully accept the fact that they may not get anywhere, but they keep on talking. It's part of the job.

Heath Macquarrie is a consistent user of the "late show" where a Member gets 7 uninterrupted minutes at 10:00 p.m. to pour out his ideas. It doesn't bring direct results, and only a few people listen, because the quorum rule is not enforced. But there are some rewards. "Occasionally your complaint catches the poor guy on night shift from Canadian Press," says Heath, "and you get a story next day."

Something of a feud developed between Macquarrie and Postmaster General Eric Kierans in 1970 and 1971. Heath raised one complaint after another about the operation of the post office department. Kierans did not have a parliamentary assistant, and had to show up himself for the late night show. And he didn't like it very much. As both Members were very articulate, the exchanges were worth staying up for. Names were coined at a high level. Macquarrie became the Merry Monk of Hillsborough; then the Faltering Falstaff of the Tories. Privately, Kierans finally referred to him as "that red-faced little bastard."

Macquarrie was annoyed.

"I'm not little," he pointed out.

But there is no doubt that the constant pressure eventually made an impact on government postal policies. In experienced hands, some benefit can be gained from the rules, once you know the limitations.

For government supporters, it's not so easy to ask oral questions or to harass ministers. "If you ask an oral question in the House," said Ken Robinson, "everyone assumes it's planted or else you're about to rebel. There's not much advantage either way." So he began to put written questions on the order paper. This way he got facts, government proposals and considered replies in writing. In fact, he raised so many questions that people began to notice. Citizens who couldn't get information from government departments wrote to him, and he got it for them. He obtained official explanations for people who felt an injustice had been done them. In a few weeks, he got statistics for small companies which had been trying for a year. Some hadn't even got a reply to their request. And none of it was secret or confidential. He was using the facilities for private Members to provide a public service.

"Everybody outside the civil service thought it a great idea," said Ken, "except my own weekly newspaper. They thought I should have more questions about Lake Shore riding."

Maybe they had something, for Ken Robinson didn't quite make it in the 1972 election. But in the four years he was there, he didn't fret about his law-making impotence. He found another function.

Barry Mather knows the facts about private Members' motions, but he keeps putting them in anyway. Once he got satisfaction of a sort. On May 8th, 1972 his resolution urging the government to initiate an Opportunities for the Aged program came up for discussion. Between 5:00 and 6:00 p.m. it was debated. Then it dropped to the bottom of the list after being "talked out." It was buried beneath 50 others. But just two hours later, John Turner presented his first budget as Minister of Finance. It included opportunities for the aged. Naturally, Barry Mather wasn't mentioned. It's not even likely Turner knew of his motion, for ministers let the Members play their little games by themselves.

"I felt like a distant relative watching the graduation," remarked Barry, deriving some satisfaction from the result.

I guess I didn't mention my own little moment of triumph. In

1961, Donald Fleming brought in a bill as Minister of Finance for loans to small businesses. Noting that it would include tourist operators, he added: "This will make the honourable Member for Parry Sound-Muskoka happy."

It did, and so did the recognition. If not father of the bill, at least I was god-father. It was the only such public acknowledgment I can remember in 15 years of trying. But then, the last nine years were in opposition, and ministers don't boost opposition Members.

In four years, Doug Hogarth, Member for New Westminster got the drift of things. He dropped out in 1972.

"What the private Member gets as a law-maker," he concluded, "is a fast ride on a square-wheeled chariot."

THE MASTERS

"They Are Unbeatable"

The peals of laughter from the government side were not exactly what Lester Pearson had expected. The newly elected Leader of the Opposition blushed and glanced over quickly at Jack Pickersgill, who sat staring grimly ahead. Then he turned toward the hoots of derision coming from the C.C.F. ranks. They were ominous. He had rather expected shocked silence from the government and serious reflection from the others. But all he was getting was ridicule.

Pearson was in a tough spot. He had to propose non-confidence in the minority Conservative government, but did not want to defeat it. A new election now, in January 1958, would be unpopular, and he would be blamed for causing it. He was also aware that the popular swing was toward Diefenbaker. Above all, he needed time to get organized. If he could only be certain what the C.C.F. would do, it would be a lot easier. They might possibly support him and vote the government out.

Yet Pearson had no alternative but to attack. Anything else would look pretty weak on his first day as leader. So he had to condemn the government in his speech and propose some kind of censure. We had all wondered what he would do.

When it came, his motion looked good on paper. After condemning the Conservatives for bad management in their seven months in office, he proposed they resign and turn the government over to him without an election. It was quite clever. No matter what way the vote went, he couldn't lose. Defeat of the resolution would leave things as they were. If it carried, he was Prime Minister. But the bright idea back-fired. Incredulous Members laughed, and so did the public. Just seven months before, Canadians had thrown the Liberals out. Now they wanted back in without even an election. That surely proved how arrog-

54

ant they were, and Pearson had turned out no better than the others. His motion was defeated. With only 112 of 265 seats, the government was safe.

Pearson's dilemma was my first introduction to the strength of the government in power. It pushes ahead, saying to one and all: "Defeat us if you dare." When the government has only minority support, the smaller parties keep it in power. They have benefited from public indecision between the two major parties, and could lose out in a new decisive election. With majority support, the government's own Members keep it in power. Many have swung in with the party, and have no desire to vote themselves out again.

When a government loses a vote in the Commons, it has presumably lost the support of the people. Custom requires that it resign and call a new election. With such dire results, its own supporters don't have much choice. Without knowledge of how other parties and other Members may vote, no Member wants to be the one to defeat his party. So they stay in bondage, and the government has its way.

So what keeps the opposition from being swept to oblivion every time a new law is introduced? The only defence is delay. To prevent a vote is the same as winning it.

The most determined effort in years was made during the debate on a national flag in 1964. "The red ensign or nothing," was the motto in one camp. "Anything but the red ensign," pledged the other. "Something nice in red, white and blue with a maple leaf," said those who just wanted a new flag.

Early in the year, Lester Pearson showed some reporters a design that appealed to him. That started the fireworks. The red ensign group then made a decision to stall until the government gave up. The debate began in early summer. The more determined the opposition became, the harder the government held out. No summer recess was proposed, but that didn't deter anyone. The session stumbled on into fall. September, October and November passed, and still the House was deadlocked. There were amendments and sub-amendments. The matter went to a committee and came back again without any agreement. As the year-end approached, nobody had won the battle. But in mid-December, when the public had become weary of the argument, the government used its final power. It chose its design, cut off debate by closure, and forced a vote. When the chips were down, the government won.

Sometimes, however, time is limited. Early in November 1966, it looked as if John Diefenbaker really had the government on the ropes. By procedural delays, he stalled a vote of money to the government. It had to have that money, and by the 10th of the month. Otherwise it could not pay its bills and would be in serious trouble. The deadline arrived with debate still in progress. Could stubbornness in Parliament, aided by government carelessness, bring it down?

Not at all. The executive power once again flexed its muscles. Digging around in items already passed, it diverted $55 million which had been voted for other purposes. "After extensive work in treasury," announced Prime Minister Pearson, "we have found the money we need." The government didn't need parliament after all. The power was there, just waiting to be manipulated.

That's the way it always goes. Using favourable rules, exercising emergency powers, switching House business around and with a firm grip on its supporters, the thirty cabinet ministers keep the House of Commons in control. And they, in turn, feel the heavy hand of the Prime Minister.

Once in a while, though, time really does run out. In 1972 the House decided to adjourn for the summer on July 7th. An election was expected to follow shortly. There was flurried jockeying for position among ministers to get their bills passed. Finance Minister John Turner had a railway bill which might just get through. John Munro's family benefits plan had passed all stages, and was in final reading. Jean-Luc Pepin had his bill on foreign control of Canadian business well along in report stage. For various reasons, all these bills had been held up by one or more of the opposition parties. It looked as if Munro had the best chance, so he got the nod. With success in sight, time ran out. He needed just one minute past adjournment hour for final reading. But he didn't get it. "That's irresponsible conduct," he charged angrily of Paul Hellyer's refusal to extend the time. "It was a stupid bill," replied Hellyer. And it died. An election was called as expected and none of the other bills passed either.

An opposition can stall, play tricks and use the rules perversely. But how do you protest if you are a government supporter? A direct assault on your own party is dynamite; so strategy must be used. One way is to move an amendment. That's sort of a flanking movement. It lets you put forward an idea without hitting your parliamentary friends head-on. But there are dangers.

Ralph Cowan tried it in February 1968 with the broadcasting bill. He charged that the bill completely failed to deal with election broadcasts. But Judy LaMarsh, Minister in charge, paid no attention to his arguments. So he moved that the clause be reconsidered. Not one of his Liberal colleagues would step out of line to second the amendment, so Conservative Terry Nugent did. Cowan's amendment might have been defeated quietly. But some NDP Members fiendishly decided to embarrass the government and demanded a formal vote. Then they found themselves trapped. Cowan got enough opposition support to defeat the government, and that was not what they wanted. So they had to go into reverse, and vote against Cowan. His amendment was narrowly defeated.

Cowan was lucky that time. He barely escaped the horrible fate of sponsoring the defeat of his own government. A government man who gets out on that limb can expect the opposition to try sawing it off. "Brought down by its own supporter," the headlines would read of the fallen ministry. The Cowan situation was a real object lesson. His party colleagues who watched with horror decided never to get caught in that trap. So amendments from the government side are generally scarce.

I was in Britain in April 1972 when a similar situation shook Westminster. Prime Minister Edward Heath had decided to take Britain into the Common Market. One of his determined backbenchers, Neil Marten, tabled a side-swiping amendment calling for a national referendum on the issue. Though Marten had a lot of support on government benches, Heath refused to accept it. Opposition Leader Harold Wilson, whose ranks were also badly split, saw a splendid opportunity to defeat the government without taking a position. He announced his support of a referendum. For a while, Heath was in real trouble, and so was Marten. But the 70 Labour Members who supported entry were not for playing games. Roy Jenkins, Wilson's deputy leader and several shadow cabinet members resigned in protest. And then it was Wilson's turn for trouble. For some weeks, his leadership was on the line. So he had to change tactics and Marten got off the hook. But like Cowan, he squeaked out by sheer good luck.

An unhappy government man has another course. He can protest vigorously against parts of a bill, then vote in favour. Steve Otto did this on the foreign take-overs bill. He didn't like it. "The bill was put together by amateurs," he charged. "There are loopholes a mile wide," he added minutes later. "It does not answer the problem." This was followed by such a steamy blast that Eldon Woolliams called out to Jean-Luc Pepin, the Minister in charge: "You will have to take this fellow to the woodshed."

But having had this freedom for a glorious fifteen minutes, Steve came back to the pack before sitting down.

"Yes, Mr. Speaker, I am going to vote for the bill," he finally concluded, amid cheers from his worried colleagues.

Opposition Members do this, too. Straying miles from the party position to express doubts, they finally vote with their colleagues. But it's pretty hollow. And it becomes even hollower when some unpleasant fellow on the other side asks at the height of the oratory, "How are you going to vote?"

The ultimate protest, of course, is the path of the martyr, outright rebellion. Talk against the agreed position, vote against the leader and even leave the party. This is very unpleasant.

But there is an easy way. Just keep quiet. You don't have to run risks, explain your position or face unpleasantness. Merely sit in your seat, pound your desk when a colleague speaks, heckle the other side and vote with the party. It is so comfortable. You're a trained seal, but what the hell. You will get re-elected just as easily and the pay is exactly the same. The government wins anyway.

When bills finally pass the House, they go to a committee. Here, according to the theory, you sit around in an informal group of concerned Members, trying to correct the government's oversights and the errors in drafting. This is clearly explained by the minister to doubters like Steve Otto. "These details can all be corrected in the committee," he says cheerfully. "The House is only concerned with the general principle."

But the strange thing is, when they get to the committee, there really aren't any oversights or errors. It's just that the Members don't understand the problems.

I remember how pleased Stan Korchinski was in May 1971 when the committee on Agriculture accepted his proposal to redefine grain for advance payments. Though he was an opposition member of the committee, several on the other side saw the force of his argument. His amendment was accepted 13 to 9, a clean majority. Bill C239 was altered and sent back to the House for passage.

"The odd break like this makes it all worth while," said Stan. "Generally, that committee work is pretty futile."

When the grain bill got back to the House in June, Minister Otto Lang had a change to propose. Officials didn't like the Korchinski amendment. The government wanted the bill restored to its original condition before the committee tampered with it.

"To do otherwise," explained Lang, "might lead to some choices by farmers not to deliver certain grain at certain times."

That is exactly what the committee had considered. But the government had its way. When Lang's motion was put to the House, no Liberal opposed it. Where were the committee members who had backed Korchinski? Who knows.

I was a member of the committee on National Resources when Hyliard Chappell put his foot down. Clause 20 of the Canada Water Act contained some bad legal principles, and he wanted the clause changed, or withdrawn. Minister Joe Greene was present at the meeting.

"I am not disposed to withdraw the clause," he said after hearing Chappell's argument and the reply of departmental officers. But the committee was with Chappell. And they were not going to be run by government officials. So the clause was unanimously struck out. Both Chappell and I had objections to clause 28 for different reasons. He moved to alter it, and his motion was carried.

"You have to get tough on these things once in a while," said Chappell, a government supporter, as the meeting broke up.

But when the Canada Water Act came back to the House, Resources Minister Greene had his way — Clauses 20 and 28 were restored to the bill. Some minor alteration in the wording of clause 20 was a concession to Chappell's point. And you have to take what you can get. For the government has the final word.

Sometimes committees look into urgent national affairs and report to the House. It tests government ingenuity to suppress some of the adverse reports. But it does. Three recommendations on policy matters were made in 1969, while Pierre Trudeau was establishing himself as Prime Minister. Let's look at them.

First was the Newfie Bullet. The Canadian Transport Commission, J.W. Pickersgill, president, decided in 1968 to discontinue passenger rail service in Newfoundland. It was a hard decision, made easier by the swing of that province to the Conservatives in the June election. The House committee on Transport and Communications resolved in November 1968 that action on the decision be deferred. But when the committee report was presented to the House, this particular resolution did not appear. An effort by Jim McGrath to expose government meddling went on for weeks, but nothing was proven. So in March, 1969, the committee passed the resolution again and made sure it was reported. This time government house leader Don Macdonald objected to receiving the report on procedural grounds. "Then what's the point of committees?" demanded Russ MacEwan, but he only got a cold stare. After two days of argument, Speaker Lamoureux allowed the report to be presented. Four days before rail service was to end on April 5th, debate began. It ended the same day. For the government, using its power to direct House business, never called the report for discussion again. It lay dormant on the order paper until the session ended in October. In the meantime, rail service ended and the "Newfie Bullet" turned its last wheel on schedule.

Next was the report on NATO. Trudeau's position on the North Atlantic Alliance was well known. He wanted to withdraw Canadian troops from Europe. The committee on External Affairs and National Defence, after extensive travel in North America and Europe, did not agree. The Prime Minister made a public statement in April, renewing his own position. But the committee was unmoved. By mid-June, its report was ready in English, and went for translation into French. On June 26th, the report was presented, recommending maintenance of Canadian Forces in NATO. But the committee had been sand-bagged. For on June 23rd, Leo Cadieux, Minister of National Defence, acting as if the committee did not exist, announced the government's decision to cut back NATO support.

"I don't know why we spent so many months studying defence matters," complained committee member Harold Winch, noting that the government did not even wait for their report. Of course, he really did know the reason. They were not coming up with the right answer.

While these things were going on, the oil tanker Manhattan prepared for its test of Canadian arctic waters. The committee on Indian Affairs and Northern Development was alarmed at the casual reaction of the government. They visited the arctic to provide a Canadian presence when the American ship passed through. In December, they presented a report which was almost a reprimand.

"The government should indicate to the world, without delay," it read, "that vessels passing through Canada's Arctic Archipelago are under and shall be subject to the sovereign control and regulation of Canada."

The government was not accepting any rebuke from a committee, nor was it about to have that report discussed. This time they did it another way. Concurrence in the report was not moved, and no debate would be held. Every time the report was called, the chairman remained in his seat. And no one got up on his behalf. So in January, 1970, Paul Yewchuk, Conservative vice-chairman of the committee rose one day when the report was called, and moved concurrence. He pointed out that it was only by courtesy that the chairman acted. There was nothing in the rules to say who moved concurrence. After consulting precedents, the Speaker agreed that any Member could bring forward the report. So it was immediately considered. It looked as if the government had lost. But not exactly. After one day's debate it became a government order; and they never called it again. It died with the session.

Having seen what happens when government supporters become independent on committees, let's see the other side. It's a lot easier when the opposition tries pushing the government around in committee. Then everyone understands the game, and jumps in on his own side. Even the committee chairman can be impartial in an objective way. One of the worst brawls I ever attended was in the Banking and Commerce committee in November 1962. The June election had returned a minority Conservative government. The issue had been financial mismanagement. Out to discredit the government at the first meeting was a high-powered strategy team including Paul Martin, Jack Pickersgill and Lionel Chevrier, joined by new Member, David Lewis of the NDP. They did not oppose when I was elected chairman. But it was the last thing they agreed to. They moved immediately that the committee undertake a study of government financial policies. Since only the House assigns committee tasks, I ruled the motion out of order. They appealed to the committee, which was packed with opposition members. I ruled there was no appeal, except to the House.

Frustrated, they started shouting to draw press attention to their effort. Government supporters shouted back. Noisy accusations and wrangling accompanied procedural motions, amendments and sub-amendments. For half an hour it was bedlam. Finally the meeting broke up in a stalemate. The noisy crew departed, still arguing. As I gathered up my papers to leave, one person was still sitting there, stunned. "My God," exclaimed new Member Walter Gordon, "is that the way they do things around here?" Assured that it was not unusual, the board-room aristocrat walked out shaking his head. He never could understand that crazy place.

Raw power, regardless of the consequences, occasionally surfaces. The government wanted its foreign take-overs bill through committee without delay in June 1972. Dozens of organizations and individuals wanted to appear. The committee could take months, and opposition members were in no hurry. But the government majority knew what to do. On June 8th they jammed through a series of motions. They decided not to hear from the provinces, from individuals or from critic Walter Gordon. They decided to hear from Minister Herb Gray and a couple of groups. They limited the total time for hearing witnesses to five days. And when the committee adjourned, the press was waiting. "It was a madhouse in there," commented NDP member Bill Knight. "A railroad," Conservative Stan Schumacher called it. "There was some very strong feeling," admitted Chairman Bob Kaplan. But the government had its way, and the bill was through committee and back in the House in fourteen days.

Government control in committees is mainly through the chairman. Though nominally impartial, he is named by the government from among their own ranks. He directs the order of business and prepares a draft report. He is made aware of government objectives and sees that they are achieved. In emergencies, he acts under a sort of osmosis, sensing what he ought to do without being told. Most chairmen are torn between a desire to be impartial and the need to be loyal to the party.

The single exception is in the Public Accounts Committee, which examines government spending. The chairman there has for 16 years been a Member of the Opposition. This removes suspicion of interference from on high. Alf Hales has made a name for himself as chairman, watching like a hawk for carelessness. During enquiry into waste and extravagance in refitting the aircraft carrier Bonaventure in 1969, the committee felt it should go to Halifax to investigate first hand. "We're not going to run up a big bill on one of those junkets," said tight-fisted chairman Hales, "I would go if we travel in government aircraft and stay in the military barracks." This was too much for one of the committee members. "Mr. Chairman," he asked, "will we be taking our lunch pails?"

But in the other committees, the chairman has his responsibility to the government. If he doesn't live up to it, there are ways of dealing with him. David Anderson discovered this when chairman of the special committee on the environment. In 1971 he became too independent on the question of arctic oil transportation. He lost the good will of the government, and so did the committee. It couldn't get space or time for meetings. It got no new references and was not even set up the following session. Anderson himself resigned to become leader of the British Columbia Liberal party.

It's tricky when government members find themselves outnumbered at committee meetings. The chairman has to be sharp. Here's how it went on one occassion in mid-July 1973. Conservative Jim McGrath, on hand promptly with nine others, moved that a 90-day freeze on prices and wages be recommended to the House. This was party policy, opposed by Liberals and the NDP. The five Liberals present realized with a shock that they were in the minority, even with help from the two New Democrats. But two fast-thinking Liberals stalled things. They pretended to be slow. They couldn't quite understand the motion, which was presented in English. They demanded a formal translation into French. Catching on quick, Chairman Jack Cullen suspended the meeting. "We adjourned because of a technical problem," he explained later, "there was a lot of activity during that period." Liberal Keith Penner rushed out and rounded up the troops.

When things looked safe, the meeting resumed. McGrath knew he was beat. "It was a good try," he shrugged. Members who stall, and a chairman who co-operates, can generally beat off an assault until reinforcements arrive.

Trained seals can be found on committees, too. In the House and in committes, everything must ultimately bend to the will of the Prime Minister and his cabinet. Opposition parties can stall. Committees can play their little games. Individual seals can break training. But the threat of an untimely election scares hell out of everyone but the Official Opposition. The goverment can rely on the solid support of its own Members, and if they are short in numbers, some other party nervously obliges.

THE MOOD

"It All Depends On How We Feel"

A flash of light filled the Commons Chamber, revealing sharply for a brief instant the features of the Members present. Caught in the camera's official eye was the tense assembly of the 28th parliament. Prime Minister Trudeau and Opposition Leader Stanfield stared at each other across the green carpet. Cabinet ministers looked at papers in their hands, or sat quietly waiting. Members fiddled with pencils, gazed around vacantly or scratched themselves. Whatever way it caught them, they were on record for posterity.

After the flash, the mood immediately relaxed. Smiles appeared and conversation started. They began to razz George Hees.

"You hit the jackpot, George," someone called out to him, and he grinned cheerfully. He had been up and down asking questions as the photographer got ready, and the shutter caught him standing, the only person in action. For the next four years, gallery visitors were handed a descriptive folder and seating plan, with that action shot on the front, in colour.

A couple of minutes later, as the question period went on, the mood changed again. Accusing questions from the opposition brought angry or evasive answers from the ministry. The backbench razzing became unpleasant. The House was once more back to normal operations.

You get the impression from official photographs and history books that parliament is a solemn deliberative body. Far from it. Those pictures are just one frame in a news reel. Set the film in motion, and you get the real mood — angry, funny or just plain dull. Even those revered fathers of Confederation, if released from their hundred-year freeze, would probably come to life arguing. It's a place of partisan struggle, personal bias and pressure, offset occasionally by a truce. The resulting moods affect the operations. It's worth taking a look at these moods, for they have a lot to do with party loyalty.

The peace is maintained by rules. The rules are enforced by the Speaker, whose word is now final. As presiding officer, he never makes speeches, despite his title. He makes rulings. Yet there are Members who defy him if he becomes too heavy-handed. And there are Members who push him if he appears to waver. He must always retain his good humour, and hold his temper, for if he breaks, so does the House. Lucien Lamoureux, Speaker for three parliaments, has had some difficult days, but never faltered.

To prevent name-calling exchanges, one Member does not speak directly to another. He addresses the Speaker. It is a fairly successful rule, but sometimes it doesn't achieve its goal. On one occasion, Drummond Clancy was being raked over by another Member. After taking it for a while, he finally got to his feet.

"Mr. Speaker," he asked, properly addressing the Chair, "would it be out of order if I called the honourable Member a son-of-a-bitch?"

The speaker nodded his head.

"I thought so," said Clancy, resuming his seat.

Failure to address the Chair is a frequent oversight. Even experienced Members do it. But they get the same treatment from the Speaker. In March, 1973, new Member Ken Hurlburt kept saying "you" to Agriculture Minister Eugene Whelan, in asking about import tariffs on beef. Speaker Lamoureux requested a couple of times that Hurlburt address the Chair. Whelan, an eleven-year Member, joined in the fun of watching a new Member master the ropes. When Hurlburt finally made it, Whelan replied helpfully: "I think you are talking about D.E.S."

The Speaker was on his feet immediately.

"Would the minister kindly address the Chair," he instructed, making Ken Hurlburt feel a lot better.

Another rule to prevent private feuds is that a member who has the floor may not be interrupted. During his allotted time, no one can even ask a question unless he consents. This sometimes leads to a dramatic gesture which impresses gallery visitors. A prominent front-bencher rises to set something straight.

"Sit down," says the back-bench orator, waving his hand.

And the big name, knowing the rules, sinks back into his seat.

But a lot of Members keep shouting out, heckling and questioning without asking for the floor. If they are audible, the House reporters record their comments. And of course the press gallery quickly notes any smart remarks.

The House isn't intended to be a dull place for reading speeches, either. So, except for ministerial statements, the only aid to oratory is notes. This rule is often broken, for it is hard to prove whether a Member is reading a speech, or referring to notes. But one thing is firmly enforced. Remarks can not be placed on record without being spoken aloud. While the United States Congress is solicitous of its weary Congressmen, the House of Commons requires its Members to listen to every dreary word. In 1972, Solicitor General Jean-Pierre Goyer found Members laughing at his statement on the Geoffroy penitentiary release. Embarrassed, he asked that the last part be recorded without being read. "Finish reading the statement," suggested the Speaker firmly.

Which he did.

If I have implied that the government merely snaps its fingers to get its way, I take it back. The House must be coaxed. It moves with a very fluid temper. Only those who spend a lot of time there can understand it. Like a grumpy husband who holds the purse strings, it knows it must fork over eventually. But it holds out until the last minute. And if the mood is bad, that can be a long time. So the government tries to keep the mood sweet, and it would dearly love to keep its own Members quiet. A misplaced comment can turn the opposition into a hornet's nest, and create an angry mood for the whole day. Norm Cafik found this out the hard way one May day in 1972.

The Prime Minister had outlined a new system of honours and awards. Bob Coates asked about an award for former Prime Minister Diefenbaker. This put something very funny into Cafik's mind. Coates had earlier written an allegory about knives in Diefenbaker's back. Now Jack Horner, Member for Crowfoot, who sat within arm's reach behind Robert Stanfield, was reportedly unhappy about his leadership. Cafik jumped up and asked a clever supplementary on the subject of bravery awards.

"Would the Prime Minister consider one for the Leader of the Opposition," he enquired, "for daring to sit with his back to the honourable Member for Crowfoot?"

The reaction was furious. Horner is not known for his good moods anyway, and he was boiling mad all day. So were all the Conservatives. Not much was accomplished in that partisan mood from 2:45 onward.

Sometimes everyone suffers from a spiteful mood. It happened that way near the end of June in 1972, when discussion of all goverment estimates was cut off at 9:45 p.m. Conservatives were annoyed about the closure rule. New Democrats were aggravated because their amendments were ruled out of order. So instead of combining the scores of items into one vote, opposition Members forced a recorded vote on each one. It looked like an all-night session. A solid government majority was present, and nothing could be gained. But on into the night went a determined House, bent on teaching the government a lesson. Around midnight, Prime Minister Trudeau, not anxious to learn any new lessons, got up and left. John Diefenbaker stayed on. During a washroom break around 1:00 a.m. someone suggested, without mentioning his 76 years, that perhaps he could go home now, too.

"I never retire," replied the former leader. As the hour got later, resistance began to falter. About 3:00 a.m. the remaining items were combined, and the government had its funds for the year.

It's fair if you wonder what was accomplished by staying up half the night. In a positive sense, nothing. In a symbolic sense, maybe something. Opposition Members could not just lie down and be trampled to death, though death was inevitable. They had to show the government it couldn't get what it wanted exactly when it wanted. Does that make sense?

The mood isn't always grim. At times it becomes quite cheerful. It takes just a word or an expression to turn the tide. Someone taking his lumps gracefully can do it. Finance Minister John Turner was being warned in mid-1972 by Robert Stanfield about the rise in the cost of living.

"His complacency is not very reassuring," commented the Leader of the Opposition.

Turner jumped to the defence. "I deny any allegation of complacency," he retorted. "This government will act when it has to."

This was not exactly the way he had intended to put it. But the words were out. He blushed slightly as Members poked fun at him, but knew better than to try correcting himself. So he sat out his discomfort with a sheepish smile.

For the next few minutes, Members kept looking at Turner and laughing. And if they caught his eye, he responded. It did no harm for the day's work. Turner was a person who made mistakes, not one of the "others."

Sometimes if the mood is good, private Members get a break too. On October 26th, 1973, without pre-arrangement or notice, Tom Cossitt proposed that the government of Cuba be asked to release Ronald Lippert from his imprisonment. "I believe the acceptance and passage of this resolution would result in his release" urged Cossitt, and he got a sympathetic response from the House. It was accepted, and passed immediately, and Lippert was home in a week.

There is often a good mood at the evening sitting after a dinner hour reception. Intoxication is not a problem in the Canadian House, but a few drinks soften the antagonism. On one occasion, a Member I prefer not to name, arrived in the House after evening proceedings had started. He flung open the curtains at the back of the Chamber, and stood surveying the scene through slightly hazy eyes. He had stayed at a reception until it was over, and hoped no one would notice that he was a little unsteady. But eagle eyes across the Chamber saw his condition at once. They also noticed something else: he had entered the wrong aisle.

"Let's give him a hand," someone said, and with good-natured malice, they started pounding their desks in applause.

The Member who was speaking looked up in surprise. He couldn't recall saying anything particularly pointed or funny. The late comer was surprised too, for it seemed they were applauding him. Trying to figure out what he had done, he made his way carefully to his second row seat, smiling and waving in reply. Arriving at his place, he was slightly annoyed to find someone else occupying it. He stood there for a moment, waiting for the intruder to leave. While standing impatiently, he noticed that the wrong person was in the next seat too. Then he realized his mistake. With remarkable presence of mind, as it seemed to him then, he turned toward the nearest person and asked a question.

"Did you enjoy the reception?"

"Didn't go," replied that honourable Member.

"Oh, I thought I saw you there."

Turning then, with great dignity, he made his way safely behind the curtains. After a decent interval, he re-entered in the right aisle. Moving carefully, he descended to his proper place and sat down, to loud applause all round. Once again the Member who was speaking had to pause, slightly irritated, until the clamour died down. Just as he began again, the new arrival remembered a traditional courtesy. He rose, bowed grandly toward the Chair and sat down again, with an air of complete triumph. Had the others not been in good humour, his condition might well have been pointed out, to embarrass both him and his colleagues. But on this occasion he was saved.

A good government house leader feels the moods, and uses them. Allan MacEachen understands them well, possibly because he is a little moody himself. House veteran John Diefenbaker not only understands the moods, he creates them. I remember one occasion when I was watching House business on behalf of the opposition whip. The Leader came in and asked what was happening.

"This bill is just about to go through," I replied. "The government has accepted some amendments and nobody else wants to speak."

"That won't do at all," he admonished. "I don't want this bill passed today."

I got up to look for some more speakers, but he motioned me down. He took his seat and listened to the debate for a few minutes. Suddenly he interjected a derogatory remark about the minister in charge. For his part, the minister would have ignored it. He had laboured hard all day to keep the House sweet; accepting minor amendments, and acknowledging criticism. But one of his back row desk-thumpers jumped to the defence. He remembered an unpleasant incident in the Diefenbaker record, and threw it back. A Diefenbaker partisan sprung up on a point of order. In a few minutes, the House had come to life — angry. Members remembered things about that bill they hadn't liked, and now wanted to say them. At adjournment, they were still talking.

In his first four years as Prime Minister, Trudeau seemed quite unconcerned about the moods he created. The opposition, he felt, was angry most of the time anyway. One day he came in for question period reading a book. It was insulting to everyone there. When he was asked questions, he half stood to answer, still reading. He seemed to be saying: "I can answer your stupid questions without disturbing my train of thought"

Finally, tired of being hassled by midgets, he picked up his book and left before the question period ended. There were no great accomplishments by the government that day.

Yet, he was often quick to respond to challenges. In April 1972, Opposition House Leader Ged Baldwin, Member for Peace River, was twitting him for not calling an election.

"When will the Prime Minister take the one major initiative to restore public confidence?" he asked.

"I would be prepared to call a by-election in Peace River," replied the Prime Minister.

And he was direct.

"What are you babbling about?" he asked Mike Forrestal, who interrupted a statement he was making.

"I'm not babbling," replied Forrestal, "you are waffling." The fast response brought a brief smile.

Sometimes he was too smart with his answers. "Bud" Simpson, Member for Churchill, Manitoba, was pressing him one day about improvements to the port of Churchill. He made no response.

"He doesn't know where Churchill is," called out heckler Don MacInnis.

"He is dead, Mr. Speaker," responded the Prime Minister.

But in Churchill, so was Trudeau. In the general election six months later, his candidate dropped to third place.

With a majority behind him, Trudeau let others worry about House moods. His own were more interesting. With the minority House that began in 1973, he was, I am told, a little more cautious.

Robert Stanfield is much more careful about moods. His penchant for calm deliberation warns him they can be destructive. Though he uses very direct language, he seldom uses provocative words. This is perhaps best illustrated by an incident during one of the Trudeau's swearing periods. The Prime Minister had angrily charged with asking a "silly God-damned question." Next day, as Stanfield got up to ask a question, he pointed an accusing finger at Trudeau.

"Don't swear at him, Bob," warned Doug Hogarth.

"No need for that," replied the Leader of the Opposition, "there are enough people in this country swearing at him already."

Rather than snapping back, Stanfield prefers to turn the smart remarks to his own advantage. Speaking on the budget debate in 1973, he asked what the government was trying to sell.

"Underwear," piped up heckler Joe Guay, referring to the family business.

"No," Stanfield replied, "they want to steal my underwear."

Tommy Douglas and Real Caouette are always in good humour. They have attentive audiences, and although they get really worked up, they do not create hostility. Nor does David Lewis, though he demands respect for himself and the House.

That reminds me of another mood that surfaces occasionally. You might call it spiteful. Members are generally good-natured with others who miss their cue to make a statement, present a report or make a speech. But there are exceptions. David Lewis, when he first came to the House in 1962, carried with him the scars of many battles as a labour lawyer. He had not become a success by easy compliance. The first few days in December, some Members thought him particularly difficult. When he failed to hear a bill called for third reading, it passed. Then he asked to revert to that item, by agreement. "No," came a chorus of injured voices. His speech was not made.

I have mentioned Joe Guay, the Liberal back-bench heckler of the 28th parliament. He was first to shout "no" when opposition Members applied for some special concession. So the situation was tailor-made in May 1972 when he missed his turn to present a report.

"I missed the call for presentation of reports," he announced. "May I have permission to do so now?"

A gleeful "no" came from several sources. And the report had to wait.

Ministers sometimes miss their turn for statements too. And if they have been miserable to someone within recent memory, they suffer for it then. The statement, of course, will be made later in the corridor. But it's another of those symbolic acts by a petulant House.

Bad moods are partisan moods. They over-ride logic, and

reason disappears. Production vanishes. But more significant, they keep the Members on their own teams — "us" against "them". Seals jump eagerly into the act. An individual is not likely to support the other side when feeling is high. The anger may turn against him. That keeps Members in line. Furthermore, government supporters who don't want to incure the wrath of the government find it best to keep quiet. Sparking a bad mood at the wrong time can be very unlucky.

THE REFORMERS

"There Must Be a Better Way"

The winter of discontent was at its peak for the government of John Diefenbaker as 1963 began. Already wracked by internal dissension over nuclear warheads for the Bomarc missiles, it received a body blow from beyond. On the night of January 30th the U.S. Department of State issued a press release contradicting statements made by the Prime Minister. This was an unfriendly act of a high order, reflecting the pressure being exerted to influence the Canadian decision.

For the Liberal opposition, however, it was a heaven-sent opportunity. The Conservative government had been reduced to a minority the previous June and a good push could put them out. Opposition Leader Lester Pearson found the position completely reversed from five years earlier. Now he wanted an election, and would welcome any issue to bring it on. The government had laid out the regular business for the next day, but Pearson wanted an immediate debate. And he found the way in Rule 26. In special cases of urgent and public importance, the Speaker could allow such a debate to supersede regular business. When the House met on the 31st, Pearson applied for leave.

Speaker Marcel Lambert, foreseeing the possibility, had refreshed his memory on the practice. He could allow a special debate if no other opportunity was imminent. His decision, according to past rulings, was final. When Pearson moved for leave, the government opposed it. Opposition Members, of course, tried to make it a national emergency. The Speaker made his decision. Pointing out that a two-day confidence motion was scheduled for the following Monday, he ruled: "This application does not meet the requirements of urgency of debate. Therefore I would not accept the motion."

This should have ended the matter. But the strategists had

expected the ruling. So they made the next move. "With regret," said Pearson, "I appeal your ruling." The Speaker was also ready for this possibility.

"There is no appeal from the Speaker's ruling," he pointed out, quoting established practise.

"Then I appeal from your ruling that there is no appeal," announced Paul Martin.

By now, all but the experts were becoming confused. Martin made strong arguments to support his right to appeal, and the Speaker knew his limitations. There was nothing positive in the rules. So he put the case to the House. The combined opposition ignored all previous decisions and voted to allow an appeal on the matter of urgency. When Pearson's appeal was put to the house, the Speaker was reversed again; not because he was wrong, but for political expediency. So the special debate was held by changing rules in the middle of the game. The Speaker was humiliated.

The question came up again six months later. The Liberals had formed a government, and Walter Gordon was in a jam with his first budget. On June 17th, Opposition Leader John Diefenbaker asked for a special debate on budget preparation under Rule 26. The government opposed it.

"There is no urgency of debate today," ruled new Speaker Alan Macnaughton, as his predecessor had done. The Conservatives accepted the decision. But not the New Democrats.

"I must regretfully appeal from your ruling," said party leader Tommy Douglas.

"There is no appeal," Speaker Macnaughton pointed out. "My predecessor so ruled on January 31st of this year."

"That ruling was reversed by the House," Stanley Knowles reminded him, "there is now an appeal."

The Speaker could not be sure whether that vote in January had actually changed the procedure, or whether it had been an exception to the rule. Deciding that the House would have to settle it, he put his ruling to a vote.

"Those in favour of sustaining the decision of the Chair will please say yea," he asked, and the yeas carried.

Gilles Grégoire was somewhat confused. "On what matter were we voting?" he asked; but nobody enlightened him. The Liberals had voted this time to sustain the Speaker, a reversal of their stand in January. And in the result, no special debate was held.

Next day, Gordon Churchill wanted to know what decision the House had specifically made. Had it sustained the Speaker's ruling that there was no urgency, or had it decided there was no appeal from his ruling? Nobody was sure. The only thing certain was that a lot of time had been wasted; a vote had been held without anybody knowing what was decided; and the House seemed to have two opposite decisions on the same rule. Procedures were in a mess.

Then and there, Alan MacNaughton decided it was time for some changes in the rules. These political appeals from decisions of the Speaker just had to be abolished. There were other things wrong too. Complaints about the question period were all too frequent. The government considered a lot of the questions frivolous. Members thought they were being cut off unreasonably. And the government had something else in mind. They wanted a procedure to bring long debates to a halt. Closure was too rough, and had been instrumental in loss of the 1957 election. Maybe something a little more gentle could be found. So Speaker MacNaughton's proposal for an overhaul of the rules was welcomed by everybody.

In December something else happened to set Members thinking. As the end of the session approached, the annual spending spree began. Every year it was the same. With time running out, great gobs of departmental spending were unexamined and unvoted. As Saturday, December 21st began, there was half a billion dollars of spending to approve in three major departmens, Health and Welfare, Public Works and Finance. But it had been a long hard year for everyone. The session which began in September 1962 had ended suddenly in an election early in 1963. Pearson's "60 days of decision" had resulted in the immediate recall of parliament after the election, and it was still going. All Members were under strain, and a break was necessary. The mood was to vote the money and prorogue that day.

Gilles Grégoire, however, proclaimed that he would not be rushed. He had quite a lot to say on the Finance estimates, which the government was holding until last. It was necessary, he assured everyone gravely, to explain once again how Social Credit policies could save the nation. And with the House in Committee, there was no limit on the number of times he could speak. He could hold things up until Sunday; and he would if he felt like it.

A feeling of desperation hit the other Members. Train and plane reservations would have to be cancelled, and it was doubtful they could be replaced. Members from far East and far West might not even make it home for Christmas.

The presence of hockey great "Red" Kelly on the government back benches gave someone a bright idea. About 3:00 p.m. at great expense, two rare front row tickets to the hockey match in Montreal that night appeared on Grégoire's desk. He had until 4:30 to catch the train. Word spread around. Members sat at their desks, stood behind the curtains, paced the lobby, watching nervously for some reaction from Grégoire. But he said nothing; and did nothing.

At 4:00 p.m. he got up and went out. Someone followed to make sure he was gone. But he only went to the washroom. On his way back, he talked to some Members standing around about the long speeches he intended to make. Was he serious or playing everyone along?

At 4:15 p.m. he got up again, causing sidelong glances in his direction. But he just went to get a book from the Table, and sat down again.

At 4:25 he left his seat and went over to speak to Minister of Finance Walter Gordon. Then he wished some colleagues a Merry Christmas and was gone. This time he left the building and took the train. The Finance estimates came up at 5:00 and were completed by 6:09. After dinner, and the closing formalities, the session ended at 11:00 p.m. Everyone got home for Christmas. But as they sped homeward, a lot of Members wondered about it all. What skullduggery had slipped through with that half billion dollars so hastily passed? And why should one man have the power to hold up all the others on a mere whim? Surely, some changes had to be made.

A special committee on Procedure and Organization began serious work in 1964. I was a member of that committee. All the complaints about Parliament poured in. We would try to put things in order, and give all the Members a break. Philip Laundy, a procedural expert from abroad, was engaged to help the committee. It was decided to make the question period sharper. And Members unsatisfied with answers, or whose questions were ruled not urgent, could have a short debate with the Minister at the 10:00 p.m. adjournment. More departments could go to committees for study. As the work progressed, something else kept creeping in. Government members on the committee referred constantly to allocation of time of the House. Things had to be done in a more orderly fashion. Opposition members were interested, but cautious. Their only defence against government is the power to delay. But if a time period for a bill is set, the government has it in the bag.

It didn't take long for Gordon Churchill to react. After 13 years in the House, he had come to two conclusions. First, you can never trust Grits. Second, efficiency always benefits the government. So he set out to spike the allocation of time proposals.

Though Opposition House Leader, Churchill was not on the committee. But he watched every move. The first proposal was a business committee of the House Leaders. They would be asked to agree in advance on the time to be allotted for each bill. If there was not unanimous agreement, the matter would drop. It looked safe enough.

"It's a trick," said Churchill, "once we agree to two or three days on an innocent-looking bill, they will move an amendment we cannot accept. But we will be stuck with an immediate vote on it."

So the committee talked about a provision to prevent any substantial amendments being made after a time agreement.

"That won't do any good," said the House Leader when Conservative Members raised the subject in caucus, "you can never define what is substantial. Anyway, it will just be a means of squeezing us into agreements. Leaks will come out of the business committee blaming me for stalling. You won't get me in there in the first place."

The committee on procedure struggled on through 1964 and early 1965. Other events were making its work difficult. A rift had developed in the Conservative party over the leadership. By some quirk of fate, four of the five Conservative members on the committee, Balcer, Baldwin, Fairweather and myself turned out to be "rebels." The other member, Marcel Lambert was a little too obstinate, wherever he stood. So Churchill had the additional problem of not even trusting his own delegates.

In March 1965 the committee had its report ready. Time allocation had been watered down further, so that only one stage of a bill would be considered at a time. Tricked on one stage, a party could refuse a time allocation on the next. The report was presented on April 2nd, the last day of the session. Everything seemed rosy. Stanley Knowles stated that he had discussed the draft with veteran colleague Diefenbaker who found no objections. But when Speaker MacNaughton asked the House for consent to present the report late at night, Churchill was on his feet.

"I explained my views to the committee and they were rejected," he said, refusing to give the necessary consent.

"But they were accepted," I said, jumping up in defence of the report.

"They were not," replied Churchill. "That is a distortion of the truth."

Shock waves passed through Conservative ranks at this rift; but I decided nothing would be gained by an argument then. Churchill did not budge, and the new rules were not adopted. Parliament then prorogued, sending them down the drain.

Single-handed, against the Grits, against his own colleagues and possibly against his own leader, Churchill held back the approaching tide of cold efficiency.

But it was a short-lived success. In a few weeks, the House got a real shock. The government made its own proposals. And they were tough. Time allocation was included, with a provision that if unanimous agreement could not be reached,the government would set its own time. Limited to an experimental basis, they scraped through. The principle that rule changes must have unanimous consent was gone. And so was Churchill's victory.

The new rules expired when the House dissolved in September 1965. And with another minority government, Lester Pearson had no heart for another fight on the rules. A committee was set up and did a lot of work, but it was left for the new parliament in 1968 to enact them. In December of that year, a lot of new ideas were made into rules. All spending estimates and bills were sent to committees. The committee system was reorganized; to keep them fluid, membership could be changed on a few minutes' notice. Members could have a second try in the House with ideas rejected in the committee. Rule 26 was changed. Two hours' notice would be given to the Speaker, and he would then decide without debate whether there was urgency. Appeals from the Speaker's ruling on all matters were abolished.

Allocation of time, however, was still unresolved. So the new

Standing Committee was asked in 1969 to try once again. This time, Government House Leader Donald Macdonald had his instructions. Force the issue, and use the government majority if necessary. A split vote had never taken place before in a procedure committee; but that was another precedent to be changed.

"This thing has to be settled," Don Macdonald said to me after one hot meeting had decided nothing.

"But no opposition can give the government power to set the length of all debates," I replied.

"You know who will win in the end," he warned, and the cat was out of the bag.

Let's skip quickly over the summer of 1969. The government forced time allocation through committee, and then through the House by majority vote and closure. Only a quirk of fate dulled the victory. In order to use closure, they had to accept unsatisfactory wording in the rule. So they ended up with a defective product. But they won.

In 1973, the new parliament decided the rules just had to be changed. Complaints were pouring in. The oral question period and the adjournment debate were not working out.

"We are not getting a fair share," complained Creditiste André Fortin.

"The leaders have taken over the question period," said Arnold Peters. "It's no longer a period for the Members."

"The backbenchers are frustrated," said Doug Rowland, pointing out their inability to get the floor.

"The ministers should get notice of questions," suggested Allan MacEachen. "Then they could give more detailed and helpful answers."

"They are unprepared and incapable anyway," replied Ged Baldwin.

David MacDonald pointed out that the adjournment debate was now impossible, with over 70 questions piled up. The procedures, in short, were once more in a mess. The new committee system wasn't working out. Committees had too much work, and not enough time or space. Members were changed too often. The House had lost control of finances. The report stage from committees, intended to help Members, was being used by government. A new procedure for emergency debates, intended to be used on rare occasions, was being used several times daily. Private

Members' bills were still being talked out.

What had happened to all those reforms over the past ten years? Well, they didn't do much for the Members. Yes, Alan MacNaughton's determination to end political appeals from Speaker's rulings was achieved. But other ways to create confusion and waste time were found. The power of one person like Gilles Grégoire to keep everyone else waiting around to pass estimates was gone, finished by a "guillotine" procedure that cut off everyone else too. Members got a new way of examining government spending, but in the process the battle against time allocation was lost. Private Members' bills, the only legislative hope for Members, were still being talked out. Had anything been gained at all? Not very much. Maybe parliament is just a place for talking after all.

Changing the rules is a balancing act, gain something here, lose something there. But as long as nothing permits reversal of the government, it's all window dressing. Private Members will only gain their freedom when they can amend or defeat government proposals without fear of reprisals or an election. I have been saying this for years. But plenty of people oppose it on the ground that the system is more important than the individual Member.

I once got enthusiastic, though unsolicited support from the Prime Minister. In February 1968, Lester Pearson quoted me with approval when justifying his refusal to resign over defeat of a tax bill. He thought it a good idea that a government should not have to resign, merely because it was defeated. But he hadn't found the idea very palatable before that, and didn't press it afterwards. It's not really popular with leaders.

The Senate-Commons committee on the constitution recommended in 1972 a fixed four-year term for parliament. During this term, the government could be hammered all over the place, so long as it was not defeated on a deliberate vote of non-confidence. Constitutional expert Eugene Forsey sees merit in the objective but cannot accept the means proposed. E.B. Osler of Winnipeg had a resolution on the order paper for free votes in the House, followed by a motion of confidence if the government were defeated. This would allow a Member to vote against a government bill, but still express general confidence in its policies. Osler is no longer in the House, but perhaps someone else will push it.

Arnold Peters admits he is not an expert on the constitution or the rules of procedure. But in his own way he has come, like a Charles Dickens character, to two tentative conclusions.

"It might be a good idea to have nothing in parliament except the question period," he mused during the 1973 debate on procedures of the House. Silly? Well, that's the best way of exposing government to the public. And most other work is just follow the leader. He wasn't too impressed by all these rule changes either.

"The rules should remain as they are so I can use them, break them or whatever suits my purpose at the time," he proposed, "if we keep changing them, it makes it more difficult for me."

And here everybody thought they were helping him. You cannot wave these thoughts away, for they were formed after 16 years of successfully using rules, breaking them or whatever suited his purpose.

Reformers will always be fiddling with procedures. But there is only one acid test of rule changes for the private Member. Does it give him genuine freedom to impose his own honest opinion? Unless it does, the seals only acquire a new routine on the same old stage. Nothing much has passed the test to date.

THE OMBUDSMAN

"Keep an Eye on the Bureaucrats"

There is a story about the late Tom Kennedy, a hard-bitten farmer, Minister of Agriculture and for six months Premier of Ontario. Receiving a delegation of fellow farmers who expected support for a government subsidy, he told them: "Look here boys, a subsidy is just giving you back your own money. When governments handle it, a big chunk disappears somewhere. So why don't you just manage among yourselves."

That was only 25 years ago. But Thomas L. Kennedy must have been the last politician to say no. Since then, a zooming number of public employees labour at giving back their own money to millions of Canadians who fondly believe it belongs to someone else.

It's an old complaint that the bureaucracy is getting out of hand. But now it's so well in control it doesn't even tell us how well. "Secret" is stamped all over documents which might reveal its methods or mistakes. Bunglers are kept anonymous, and go right on bungling, in the same job or somewhere else. We don't even know how many there are. In 1971, according to the Public Service Commission, there were 216,488 federal government employees. A parliamentary return said about 266,000. Spending estimates showed 286,976, and the Bureau of Statistics said 402,079. Of course, each agency figured it on its own basis. Take your choice.

The service is growing faster than the population. In Tom Kennedy's day, there were 7 federal employees serving every thousand Canadians. Now there are 13. But no matter how many, we keep asking for more. They are doing what successive groups of Canadians have demanded — collecting our money, and handing part of it back. And they are protecting themselves while doing it.

One way of keeping the public and their Members from learning too much is to constantly reshuffle departments,sections, branches and agencies. And always in the shuffle, they manage to grow bigger. Here again, you can take your choice in figures. The estimates 25 years ago provided for 30 departments and sections. Now it's 90.

Let's finish with figures by looking at what a Member has to cope with in Ottawa. Just ten years ago, government occupied 10 million square feet of space in the national capital region. Now it's 25 million. Old buildings come down, larger ones go up; parts of a department move, parts stay. Sections of government are transferred from one department to another. Some go into temporary rented space; others into a new building complex. Entire new communities, miles apart, have spread government all over the Ottawa-Hull landscape.

So what? Provincial and municipal government is growing even faster. It's the same all over the world. The point is that nobody knows what's going on any more. The Members lose track of which Minister is responsible for what; the minister can't keep track of what is going on in his department; and one department has no idea what the others are doing. When something goes wrong, it's a mess. But Members must try to keep this immense system straight, and know where to turn when something goes wrong.

Trying to keep a finger on the bureaucrats is a full-time job. When a Member gets out of the House to escape the confusion, he goes to his parliamentary office and finds more. Let's look at the way some of his office problems develop.

Gordon Arnold Lonsdale left Canada with his mother in 1932 at the age of 8. She was returning home to Finland after ten unhappy years in Canada. They both disappeared, presumably dead, somewhere in Eastern Europe. In 1954, a Soviet spy showed up in Kirkland Lake, Ontario, where Lonsdale was born, claiming to be Lonsdale. Fully briefed on everything known about the boy, he obtained a birth certificate. Armed with this, he obtained a Canadian passport. It was authentic, and contained the picture and signature of the spy.

In 1955, the new Lonsdale arrived in England, and for five years directed a high level spy ring. Finally detected, he was tried and sentenced to 25 years after a sensational 1961 trial. After a couple of years he was exchanged and returned to Russia, where he died without revealing his true identity. That he was another person, and not the real Lonsdale, was proven by some interesting detective work. While checking the medical records, police found the child had been circumcised when a few days old. The spy was not.

The case was embarrassing to the Canadian government, and it re-examined its procedures for issuing passports. But officials decided that the Lonsdale case was so exceptional that no reasonable precautions could have prevented it. It took another bit of international embarrassment to jolt the department into action. In 1968 civil rights leader Martin Luther King was assassinated in the United States. When James Earl Ray was finally arrested and charged with the crime, he was reportedly in possession of two Canadian passports. They had been issued on false information, but were real passports. Charges were laid against a travel agent for signing the declaration. But this did nothing to remove the stigma of poor passport control. So the government ordered imposition of severe new regulations on June 23, 1969. Applicants born outside Canada had to provide a certificate of citizenship. New identification was required. Old passports were not renewed. If a question was not clearly answered the officer had to assume that another Lonsdale or Ray was concealing information.

The foul-up which resulted is hard to imagine. Most applicants were about to travel abroad, and had their plans all made. The delay while applications were sent back and forth got people worried. Soon there was a big back-log of unprocessed applications. As departure day approached, travellers had no passport. They wrote and got no reply. They tried to phone but the lines were all busy. In the department, experienced passport officers were diverted to search for last-minute files, and green staff was taken on. Over in the Citizenship office, an increase in urgent applications slowed things down. The system became paralyzed. People then thought of their Member of Parliament. The mess was in Ottawa and so was he. For nearly two years, until passport issuance smoothed out, Members and their secretaries spent many long hours getting constituents off on their trips. It was running so close that Air Canada had a special service from Ottawa, in which passports were delivered to travellers at the airport of departure. It was hectic.

There were other citizenship problems, too. One of the most unusual was that of Mrs. Margaret Eisdness. She was born in Canada and lived here all her life. Her family had been Canadians for several generations. Just after the war ended in 1945, she married Ivar Eisdness, a Norwegian service man who decided to stay. He eventually obtained citizenship. But when they applied for passports to visit Norway in 1972, Mrs. Eisdness was refused because she was a Norwegian. Her husband got his because he was a Canadian. Prior to 1947, a wife acquired the citizenship of her husband, so she became a Norwegian when she married him. But when he became a citizen, the law had changed. She was still Norwegian and he a Canadian. It was straightened out by filing a declaration of intention, and she once more became a Canadian. Her passport was issued and they got away for Norway just in time.

Members frustrated by efforts at law-making often find the role of expediter more satisfying. A distressed constituent who gets help in time of trouble doesn't forget. The Member becomes acquainted with departmental practices and people. And there is plenty of opportunity.

The passport fiasco was still at its height in the winter of 1970-71 when the unemployment insurance crisis began. For several years, the Commission had been consolidating and centralizing its claim-paying system. Suddenly it became overloaded. The computers couldn't handle the load, partly from bad management, partly from human error. Cheques for some unemployed persons did not arrive for weeks after they were approved. The Commission offices were flooded with calls; lines were busy; everyone was impatient. Once again, the Members had to intervene. The next winter was even worse. With the computer already showing signs of indigestion, a new Act was brought into force. New rates, new benefits, new qualifications and new forms all helped to snarl up the system. Morning and night, in Ottawa or at home, Members were besieged by impatient callers. The Members got some of the blame and abuse too. They were the visible representatives of government, and could not hide, close the doors or remain anonymous. It was a disaster. These were two situations where Members became expediters on behalf of their constituents. There are dozens more. People now expect their Members to smooth out the operation of the laws they have passed. Each person is a special case. He does not understand the laws, the regulations, how they came into being or how they are applied. But he expects his Member to. And he expects a favourable decision.

Federal Members only recently got into the wholesale business of mediator between constituent and government. Formerly they were mostly concerned with general policies. The era of minority government which began in 1957 (5 out of the last 7 parliaments) brought on a more personal appeal to voters: "I can do something for you." At the same time, and not completely unrelated, federal government got into subsidy programs and social welfare schemes, where everyone wants his grab at the bag. This multiplied the number of people who figured they got a raw deal. But when they try now to get redress, they find the public service a closed shop. "You do not qualify under the regulations," is about all they can find out. Errors, delays and bad judgment in departmental decisions result in a closing of ranks. The constituent then turns to his Member to sort it out. That Member's presence in Ottawa and his familiarity with the administration is essential. For the civil service is a hard nut to crack.

A personal incident illustrates the first problem. At a committee meeting studying Public Works spending in May 1972, I asked how much space the government occupies in the Ottawa-Hull region. "We can obtain this for you," replied Minister J.E. Dubé. "None of my officials have that on hand right now."

Prodded for some idea of the last ten years' increase, deputy minister John A. MacDonald took a guess. "Accommodation will follow growth of the public service, which has been about 1.8 per cent per year," he said.

Three weeks later, I got a letter from the Minister. It gave the figures I have already quoted near the beginning of this chapter, 10 million square feet in 1962, 25 million in 1972. An increase of 150 per cent rather than 18. The information was so shocking that the letter was marked "personal and confidential." It could not, of course, have that character, because it was information promised at a public meeting of a parliamentary committee. But it illustrates the practice in government to mark "confidential" or "secret" on anything it doesn't want out. Within the service, that marking demands absolute compliance.

Kildare Dobbs, a Canadian writer, was employed for a while in the Secretary of State's office. He was amazed how the words rattling loose in his head became confidential the moment he wrote them down.

"A few strokes of the borrowed ball point and presto! I was spinning state secrets out of my own innards," he said later. "With superfluous caution, they put up a smokescreen of security, mindlessly stamping everything on their desks, Top Secret, Eyes Only, Secret and Confidential."

This is the kind of security wall the citizen can't penetrate on his own. It's not too easy for his Member, either. But he has a better chance.

Within the outer wall of secrecy, there is an inner one I will call chain-of-command. The public service is a para-military organization. You never complain over your immediate superior, and never, never to a politician. "It is unforgiveable for bureaucrats to give information to Members of Parliament which might undermine the government," warned bureaucrat-politician J.W. Pickersgill during a lecture in Ottawa in 1972. Particularly if it's a Liberal government.

It's even more dangerous if you are a member of the RCMP, a federal force. Former Corporal Jack Ramsay made some revelations after leaving in 1972. "A member of the force could never talk to a Member of Parliament for fear of being charged and sentenced to a maximum of one year's imprisonment," he said.

This explained something I had noticed a couple of years earlier. Several of us went curling one night in a rink frequented by the public service. Short two curlers, we picked them up in the ante-room. After listening to the conversation for a couple of ends, the spares came to a conclusion.

"These guys are Members of Parliament," one Mountie was overheard telling the other. "Let's get the hell out of here."

And with hasty apologies, they left.

But the ultimate sin for anyone in the federal service is to express opinions publicly. Most everyone in Ottawa knows about John Kroeker. A high-salaried actuary in the Department of Insurance, he was horrified in 1965 over the proposed Canada Pension Plan. Actuarily a nightmare, as social welfare a failure, Kroeker spoke up about it in the department. Though some agreed, nobody wanted to say anything. Convinced that nobody in the public service was going to express any doubts whatever, Kroeker finally did, publicly.

"I don't want my children to bear that burden," he said. He was promptly fired. Not only that, retirement benefits were withheld. I had a lot of admiration for a man with a large family who laid his job on the line for a principle. But efforts to help him were hopeless. He had offended the minister in charge, Judy LaMarsh. He had broken the code of monastic silence in the public service. He is still struggling along, outside the service, making known his well-reasoned views on public affairs.

If there is validity to my theory that Members are trained seals, I don't know what I would call the individual public servant. His freedom of independent expression is just nil. Yet he gets his revenge in his own way. Over the past couple of years, a lot of so-called secret documents and information have leaked out. In most cases, it happens when the government is saying or inferring something inaccurate. It only takes a minute for someone to photostat a document and put it in the mail. It's just too bad John Kroeker had to be punished for taking up his case openly.

Appointments to jobs in the public service still see some funny work. It used to be blamed on the Members; but everything has now been taken out of their hands and left with the Public Service Commission. But that didn't end the patronage. It just put it in other hands. Now, specifications for jobs are written up so that only the person they want can qualify. In one case I pursued, an applicant they wanted could not qualify. So the Commission opened a new competition, properly worded, and appointed her under the new circular. No appointment was made under the first one. Trying to pin that "case" down was like "nailing jelly to the wall." I don't imply that this is general practice. But it happens enough that people take a chance, and complain to the Members of Parliament from within the service. And there are plenty of complaints from the public, too.

In dealing with the bureaucracy, lack of communication is often as big a factor as secrecy. Government is a gigantic set-up, and few people really know its detailed operation. Regulations are followed, policies are observed, and rulings made without too much attention to individual cases, or even to what others are doing. Once made, decisions are backed up all along the line, until someone from outside, like a Member, forces reconsideration. It's too much trouble to reverse the man on the spot. Public servants are inclined to think of Members as faceless characters trying to get special treatment for friends. Some Members consider public servants faceless characters who sit in their offices making bureaucratic decisions without knowing the facts of life. Good communication is the answer to this problem, and it's up to the Member. He won't find a public servant coming to him. But he generally finds a good response and a reasonable attitude when he makes a personal request.

"You should see the condition of some of these wharves," I said on the telephone to R.P. Henderson, district engineer of the Department of Public Works, a few years ago.

"I'd like to," he replied. "When do you have a couple of days?"

Right then we set a date, and he came up to the riding. By car, motor boat and on foot, we looked over the problem areas together. I told him what the people wanted. He told me what he could do, given the time and money. After that, we each knew what the other was talking about.

"I don't know enough about the Georgian Bay coast," I admitted to Dick McKean one day when we were discussing aids to navigation.

"Why don't you go out on the service ship?" suggested the District Marine Agent. "You can take your wife along. You will have to pay for your rations, but we have good accommodation on the Alexander Henry." And after three days, I knew something about the Georgian Bay navigation facilities.

Another excellent source of communication is between Members and government field workers. They have a lot in common. Both work at the dirt level of government, in direct contact with unhappy, bitching, improvident and neglected Canadians. Often they visit or hear from the same people and get two different stories. A little direct communication can prevent an unnecessary fight in the Minister's office over whose word to accept. Some Members don't have the time or take the trouble, and it is their loss.

Probing the administration is difficult, what with secrecy in government, a silent public service, closed ranks when mistakes are made and a lack of communication in several directions. But a Member has one advantage, a public platform. The possibility of him delving into, and disclosing, more basic secrets often persuades government to give out lesser ones. Most information isn't really that secret anyway, when they look at it closely.

For some years, there have been proposals to appoint an ombudsman in Canada. This is an officer who investigates and reports on complaints against the public service. At the moment, we have 264 people doing this job, in his or her own particular way. Until someone decides that they can be more usefully occupied, one more isn't going to help very much. Furthermore, some Members like being an ombudsman. It gives them a feeling of satisfaction and importance to right wrongs and give the public a break. It compensates a little for the discouragement of House business. And it helps them get elected again.

THE NEW LIFE

"I Like It"

When a person is elected to Parliament, he gets much more than a new job; he starts on an entirely new life. His place of business moves two hundred or two thousand miles away. His own community and his own home are no longer havens from the world outside. He is on call 24 hours a day. There are compensations, but these only make the change more positive. He is a local celebrity, a person of influence when home. He travels continually, in his riding, to Ottawa, throughout Canada and occasionally abroad. He is constantly busy.

"Politics is best suited for two kinds of people," Paul St. Pierre said a couple of years ago, "young, unmarried, intelligent men in their twenties, or men near retirement but still active. In between, it's no good."

But the vast majority of new Members in Canada belong to the "in-between" group. They are married men in their thirties and forties with growing families. And so the first decision to be made is whether the family moves to Ottawa or stays put. It's a difficult decision. I often think of Alex Macdonald, a British Columbia friend from law school days. Alex was elected in 1957. The House met in October and the family decided to look for a home in Ottawa. Finally finding what they wanted, his wife and daughter moved. Within days of getting settled, early in 1958, parliament was dissolved and Alex was back campaigning in Vancouver. When the election was over, he had been defeated. He never returned to Ottawa, except to pack.

Paul St. Pierre must now be impresed with the wisdom of his own words. Elected from British Columbia in 1968, he lived alone in Ottawa for the first two years; then his family moved to the capital. But it didn't work out. He saw them little more than if they were back home. After a year, they returned to British Columbia.

They were reconsidering at the time the 1972 election was called. But Paul was spared any further decision; he was defeated.

I have another friend from B.C., John Fraser, who was elected in 1972. Ottawa seemed perfect for wife Cathy, a native of nearby Carleton Place. But after adding everything up, they decided not to move. John got home to Vancouver occasional week-ends and spent all his time rushing around the riding.

After daughter Sheena asked plaintively, "Why does daddy bother coming home if we never see him?" they decided to be with him in Ottawa. In August 1973 they moved.

A wife at home actually becomes something of an assistant Member. That is both good and bad. It's good for the public and for the Member. It keeps him in touch with his riding. But it's bad for her. Answering the telephone and the door, taking messages, guessing when he'll be home and what he will do, filling in at public events and wedding anniversaries keeps a woman with a family pretty busy. Her duties don't end when her husband gets home either. A couple of years ago, Norman Williams, husky chief of an Indian band some distance away called at our house near noon. As he was leaving, I could smell food cooking, so I asked him to stay for lunch. There is always enough for one more. He hesitated. "Well, no, I guess not," he finally said, "we should get back home."

After he left, Marie had a question. "It was nice of you to ask Norman," she said, "but did you know there were five others sitting out in the car?"

There are advantages in moving to Ottawa. About a third of the wives do. It saves a lot of the weary travelling an anxious husband and father must do. Free of local obligations, weekends can remain a family time. Horizons broaden for wife and children. In recent years particularly, Ottawa has become a pleasant place to live. In the mid-fifties it was pretty much a dull provincial city. Downtown was a collection of ancient office buildings and brick residences, disturbed only by the trains rolling into Union Station and street cars rumbling by. But now it has come to life. Office towers, attractive new hotels, exciting places to dine, dance and drink have appeared. Boutiques and craft houses give the shopper interesting choices. The trains and street cars have gone. Sparks Street has become a pedestrian shopping mall equal to any in the world. The National Arts Centre has risen in city centre, bringing music and drama to the capital. There has been a change in spirit too. Off-beat shows, outside art exhibitions and youth festivals are encouraged. More of the French influence is evident. The hippie invasion was well handled, and the young people contribute to the good spirit. Moving to Ottawa is no longer a drag.

A few years in Ottawa is broadening for children, too. The French fact in Canadian life becomes evident for families from English-speaking communities. The operation of government is seen close at hand, as part of every day life. National figures are seen live, as people. The way children casually accept dad's important friends was brought home to Tom Bell a couple of years ago. Cy Kennedy, a former Member from Nova Scotia, called at the house to visit the Bells when in Ottawa. Tom introduced Cy to the family as Mr. Kennedy. He lost an arm in the war, and children are fascinated by this peculiarity. Young Andy Bell was no exception. He followed Cy around the house, intrigued. Later he was overheard telling a friend, "I thought President Kennedy was dead, but he isn't. They only shot his arm off."

Maybe you wonder about those Members who, after ten or fifteen years of married life, suddenly find themselves living alone in a bachelor apartment in a trange city. What do they do in their spare time? It's an interesting thought. The first thing to remember is that they are scared to death of getting caught at anything improper. The supposedly staid Britishers, with one sex scandal after another, don't let them forget the dangers. It's sudden death in politics. While researching this aspect of public life, I recently came across the book called *Sex and the Public Service* 1969, by Kathleen Archibald. The title looked promising. So I got it. But like so many other things in public life, it was disappointing. It turned out to be a report on the relative number of males and females employed in the public service, broken down by type of work and department. Opportunities to relieve the boredom of a life devoted to the people? Application forms for another job. Positions described? Try another department. On the general subject, I'll have to leave you guessing, the same as I do.

There have been a few incidents around the buildings. Every now and then a female gets on staff with more than typing on her mind. And she finds takers. On one occasion, a couple of Mem-

94

bers got the idea there was something going on between a colleague and another Member's secretary. They decided to have some fun, and end it at the same time. Waiting until things had become quiet behind the locked door, they threw a metal wastebasket through the open window from an adjacent office. Then they strolled back through the inner corridor to see what happened. They were just in time to see the victim making a hasty exit. He knew he had been found out, and never went there again.

Quite aside from Ottawa, life is different in the home community and around the riding. The former private citizen has become a local celebrity. Prime Minister Pierre Trudeau once said that when Members get 50 yards from parliament hill, they become nobodies. He said it in a fit of annoyance, but as a general statement, he had it all wrong. The fact is that when most Members leave parliament hill and return home, they become somebodies. Not lumped with 263 others in the Chamber, each Member is the federal presence in his own riding. He is a political authority, socially acceptable and the only one of his kind in the area. He goes to a lot of social events, wedding anniversaries, official openings, annual meetings and turkey dinners. With no obligations except to "say a few words," these are the happiest parts of many Members' lives. They were for me. Sitting at the head table of an agricultural society dinner, a tinge of autumn in the air, the smell of coffee from the kitchen and with happy people chattering all around, I would feel a great affection for that place and those people. I remembered other events in this hall, other visits to this community. Festivals, fall fairs, meetings, winter carnivals, stop-overs at the hotel, door-to-door canvasses, local problems solved, all flashed back with great warmth. I realized I was an honoured part of the community, an accepted element of the life here.

The feeling inevitably poured out with my few words, and I could feel the response. Driving home afterwards, all the problems and pressures would disappear, and suddenly it would all become worth while. Sometimes I wondered if there wasn't something emotionally out of place in these feelings. But I found that other Members have them too. That's what really keeps them going.

"The truth is," wrote Gordon Fairweather in a MacLean's

magazine article in January 1973, "I am engaged in a passionate love affair with people and places in the area I represent in parliament."

That's what I mean. And when that love affair develops, the partners are not easily separated. It's not all sentimental. Sometimes hilarious things happen to provide memories. In September 1971 I went to an outdoor turkey dinner near Emsdale with Lorne Maeck, now provincial member for Parry Sound. Everything was spread out buffet style. A heavy-set visitor went and got his plate of turkey and the trimmings, but when he sat down at an empty table to eat, it tipped over. His plate went flying.

"Never mind," said the hostess, "there is plenty of food. Start again."

So the hungry visitor took another helping. Thinking that the table had been slanting the wrong way, he sat at the other side next time. But he was wrong. The table was light and unstable, and he was heavy. Over he went a second time, along with his plate of food. People started to laugh. The hostess rushed over again, and said as sincerely as she could, "I really am sorry. It's our fault. Come and get another plate."

Once more, looking a bit sheepish, but acting like a good sport, the unlucky man took a full helping. This time, however, he avoided the scene of his misfortunes. Finding a vacant spot at the centre of a long table, he carefully set down his plate. Waving blithely to the hostess, who watched anxiously, he started to sit down. It was all too much for the man seated across from him, who got up to laugh somewhere else. The two covered tables, set end to end, immediately changed position, and the table cloth buckled. Turkey, cranberries, turnip, dressing, potatoes and gravy slid to the ground. Now the whole crowd was laughing. They watched to see what he would do next.

"Oh, shit!" he exploded as he stomped off to his car. And it didn't even sound vulgar.

The local celebrity who diligently goes out to meet his people has one real problem, and that is remembering names. Faces are familiar and names are familiar. The difficulty is putting them together instantly. It's often made worse by the warmth of the encounter. Pleasant memories are associated with that face, but the place and name are shrouded in a great fog. Hoping for a lead from the conversation, the Member keeps digging himself in deeper.

Everyone has the problem, everyone finds his own solution. Some are quite good at it, but there are numerous stories of people who got caught. My favourite is about Paul Martin, long-time Liberal Member for Essex East, who never forgets a face, and never misses an opportunity. In the early sixties, several Windsor area Members arrived home together, and were waiting briefly at the airport for a ceremony to begin. Among them were Paul Martin and Conservatives Dick Thrasher and Ernie Campbell. Paul spied familiar faces in the crowd and hastened over to talk to two ladies. After a brief conversation, he rejoined the others.

"Paul, I bet you haven't the slightest idea who those ladies are," said Dick Thrasher, teasing him a bit.

"I most certainly have," replied Paul indignantly, "they are great supporters of mine. One of them ran a committee room for me in the last election, and the other is one of my poll captains."

"Well that's very strange,"said Dick, "because one is my wife and the other is Mrs. Ernie Campbell."

The new life sharpens up considerably when a Member begins to travel throughout Canada and abroad on parliamentary business. More and more committees are touring Canada to reach the people. Personally, I never made one of these travelling acts. But I came pretty close once. A member of the Northern Affairs committee for about ten years, I had another Member take my place on one occasion when I was away. At that very meeting the committee decided to tour the North; it also determined that the only persons eligible to go were members of the committee at that moment. So I lost out. But a couple of months later I did get to Frobisher Bay with Nordair, the private line that services the area.

But it's the trip abroad that really extends horizons. Selection as a delegate to an international conference is a real prize. And party representatives decide who will go on the party's allotment. This isn't overlooked when a Member adds up the cost of becoming an internal nuisance.

I suppose a trip to the United Nations rates highest. New York is only 75 minutes by air from Ottawa. But an appointment as observer or delegate there is a voyage to the centre of world affairs. In spite of criticism, failures, crisis and near-bankruptcy, the world body plods along. It has lasted now much longer than many dared hope. One of the most moving events I ever witnessed was in the great assembly hall during the memorial service for Secretary General Dag Hammarskjold on September 28th, 1961. Hammarskjold had died in a crash while on a peace mission to the Congo. As the President of the General Assembly took his place, a great hush fell on the crowd. The President began the service with a solemn testimonial. Then he sat down. A second speaker followed.

"Great sacrifices will have to be made in the cause of peace," he said in English. "The way will be long and hard, and many will fall."

The tone was anxious, the words sincere. But the audience could not exactly see which of the world's great orators was addressing them. Suddenly, in the revelation of an accented word, the entire assembly recognized the familiar voice of Dag Hammarskjold himself. Incredulous listeners gasped. It couldn't be. But in a moment it dawned on them that a tape of a recent speech was being played back. Open tears replaced respectful silence. Hammarskjold was delivering his own memorial message.

Only a few Members make the United Nations delegation. But there are other opportunities. The Inter-Parliamentary Union was formed 85 years ago to provide a personal meeting place for members of the world's parliaments. About 65 countries from all continents are members. The Commonwealth Parliamentary Association is a similar body whose members and interests centre around the Commonwealth of Nations.

The North Atlantic Assembly derives its membership from countries belonging to NATO. These three hold annual assemblies throughout the world. There are also various smaller groups and parliamentary meetings, such as the Canada-U.S. annual exchange. These groups do not make binding agreements. They set guidelines and objectives for governments to follow. Before departing for conferences each Canadian delegation is brought up to date by external affairs officers, through the parliamentary centre, headed by Peter Dobell. Delegates then have sufficient background of the subject and the Canadian approach, to speak intelligently in the world council. At these conferences, Members from different political systems exchange views, person to person. They get an inside view of the way things operate in other parliaments.

I took particular interest in the Inter-Parliamentary Union, and got to three conferences. At the 1971 conference in Paris, our secretary Jean MacPherson learned that the Soviet delegation was opposing the idea of an international youth group. We wanted to know why, so I approached the head of the Soviet delegation about it. He was very helpful.

"Talk to the man in charge," he said, "I will get our interpreter to help you."

I knew the man he pointed out, for we worked in the same committee.

"Why are you not supporting the international youth group?" I asked him.

"Because we do not favour it," he replied.

"But what reason would you have?" I pursued.

There was a pause, then the Russian became confidential. "I may as well tell you," he said frankly, "it's because our delegation abstained on it at the United Nations."

"Why was that?" I asked, hoping to learn something we didn't already know.

"Because it's policy," he replied, triumphantly.

And that ended it.

Canadians sometimes reveal their own special practices to the world. That same Paris conference was opened by President Georges Pompidou in the historic palace of Versailles. A thousand delegates and their wives were jammed into the ornate auditorium an hour early. The formalities began with an address by Senator Prélot, head of the host group. He spoke in French. He outlined the history of the I.P.U. since its founding in the 19th century. On and on he went. President Pompidou's broad smile faded. Feet shuffled, and people squirmed in their seats. When he finally finished after 35 minutes, there was relieved applause. Another person then rose, and began to read the same speech in English, the other official language. For half the people there, neither language was too familiar. They could see the proceedings dragging on for hours. The Canadians knew what to do in that situation. In a bilingual House, we terminate unnecessary interpretation all the time. As the reader paused to turn a page, the solemn silence was broken by a shout from the Canadian group: "Dispense."

All eyes in the great hall turned with shock to the source of the rude noise. The interpreter faltered for a moment; then carried on. But it gave the President a way out. He sent a note to the interpreter. There was a sound of turning pages.

"And in conclusion," he began again, and the interpretation was over.

Other speeches were brief, and the assembly shortly rose. As they left, delegate after delegate came over to the Canadian group and said, each in his own language: "Thanks."

The supreme compliment was paid by an Australian. "I wish we had thought of that," he said.

When a delegation of Canadian Members goes abroad, partisan lines fade out. It is a group representing Canada. A sense of comradeship develops which carries on after the return home. Foreign policy does not divide parties as much as other things. Our external interests are governed by our geography, history, resources, products and people, much more than politics. These conferences abroad turn the pale luminaries of parliament into shining lights. Some Members become leader or deputy leader of the delegation, a real diplomatic honour. Others are Canadian delegate to one of the committees, spokesman in effect for his 22 million countrymen. At receptions and dinners, the formal old world courtesies make the delegate feel exalted. It is stimulating, but temporary.

I was leader of the 1972 delegation to Rome. When the conference was over, David Rose of the Canadian Embassy despatched us like royalty to the airport in the Ambassador's limousine. But next morning, a mix-up found Senator Joe Greene, his wife Corinne and myself bumping along in a third class railway coach in Germany, our belongings piled around us like refugees. We were trying to get to the Canadian air base at Lahr. We had carted our own luggage, rushed from track to track, changed trains on a wild guess in mid-Germany and ended up exhausted, dishevelled and hungry. We didn't look or feel much like the VIPs of the night before. But we made it. It was a symbol of the Member's life.

One day the pampered prima donna; next day an unknown wanderer.

It is all part of the new life. A Member is a local celebrity, a national figure and an international dignitary. Then suddenly he's back on the street, looking for votes like a bum scrounging cigarette butts, or sitting in the House pounding his desk and doing the trained seal act. But there is one thing the schizophrenic Member knows for sure. He would like to travel again. So would his wife. If he minds his business and works hard, fortune may smile on him once more.

THE SOCIAL WORKER

"Knock on Any Door"

Sitting at the kitchen table in an old frame house, we tried to sort things out. The room was dimly lit by a bulb suspended bare from the ceiling. The rest of the house was in darkness. Over in the corner by the wood stove, her husband sat smoking his pipe, occasionally shuffling around to carry out some chore or another. The house had a stale odour, old furniture, work clothes, drying food, cistern water and an occasional down-draft from the chimney. Overlaid was a honey-sweet smell, possibly from his pipe tobacco or from food in the cupboard.

"You don't have a birth certificate, then," I acknowledged, "but what about a marriage certificate?"

"I sent that in but it didn't do no good," replied the lady of the house. "They never even answered."

"But you must have got some letter from the department," insisted her visiting Member of Parliament. "I need letter with a number on it."

"I only got one letter, but I wrote on it and sent it back to them."

The problem was familiar. The lady wanted the old age pension, but could not prove her age. I could imagine this poor woman sitting at this very table writing that incomprehensible letter.

"Dear Sir - they won't give me my penshun. I don't think that's fair after all these years. Please make them send it to me."

I had answered, asking for a file reference or anything to locate the problem. In reply, there had come another vague letter complaining that nobody would help her. So I had put the letter in the file for the next trip to the riding. It was a slow process, extracting the information we really needed.

"Do you have a family Bible?" I asked. "There might be something in it."

"There was one. I think my brother John got it when mother died."

"Would he be there now, if I dropped in on my way home?"

"Oh, I guess so. But he goes to bed early."

Having learned everything helpful, I left to find brother John. After a lot of enquiring and with good luck, I found him and got the Bible.

Back in Ottawa with a certified copy of the birth sheet from the family Bible and all the other information, I sent off a letter to the Old Age Security Division of the Department of National Health and Welfare. In ten days a reply came.

"We now have three inconsistent dates of birth," advised the writer. "Her application form states she is 65; the family Bible indicates she is 66, but the marriage certificate shows her only 63. Perhaps a census search would help verify the situation."

A census search is the last resort. But there would be no use sending the application form to that woman to fill in by herself. She would foul it all up for sure. That meant another trip to the old home. When I got there, she had some explanations.

"I sort of fibbed when I got married," she admitted.

"My husband is a good man and I didn't want to lose him. But I was older than him, so I knocked two or three years off my age."

"How many years was it?" I asked.

"That's the trouble," she said. "I'm not sure any more. I told my wrong age so long that I can't remember the right year, exactly."

The census form was filled out and mailed. Shortly a good report came back. The census information and the family Bible were consistent. She was 66 and should have been getting old age security for a year. Proof of age was accepted and pension approved from the date of her original application.

Some time later, another of those laboured letters arrived, but this time the message glowed through the scrawled words.

"I got my cheque today for four months back," she wrote, "it will sure help. God bless you for all your good work." It brought a little lump to the throat and for a brief moment I felt it was all worth while.

Every Member goes about his job in his own way. But no matter where he sees his duty, the welfare of his constituents demands constant attention. He can go through the motions and fulfill te requirement by answering letters. For some, little more is possible because of official duties in Ottawa or distance from the riding. Others start out with enthusiasm, then begin to neglect the work as other priorities develop. The Member who constantly travels his riding, making personal calls in response to requests, becomes a social worker. And he has a most unusual status. He is field worker and head office man at the same time. In any other hierarchy it wouldn't be allowed.

Rural ridings seem best suited to bring out the social worker in Members. But not entirely. There are a few big-city Members who get elected time after time, regardless of the political swing, by becoming a riding man. They make enough calls, they do enough good work that they overcome the anonymity of city living and become a fixture among a fast-changing population.

Most of the problems would be solved if the Member could just put a ticket in the mail saying, "Give this person something useful to do and pay reasonable wages." Some people in fact seem to think that's all he has to do. Regardless of some sophisticates who disparage the so-called "work ethic," most people want to provide for themselves and their families. Instinctively they know that a bit of their self-respect disappears when they accept hand-outs. But for hundreds of thousands of Canadians, there is nothing to do. And if they can't earn money, they have to get it somewhere else. And after everything else has failed, they try their Member of Parliament. Let's look at a typical week-end.

The phone rang at seven in the morning. Still weary from the late trip home from Ottawa, I tried to focus my thoughts on the person at the other end of the line. Fumbling for a pencil, I wrote down the name, address and phone number and a few notes. I hoped I could remember later what they meant. Dozing off, I was wakened again by an insistent pounding at the front door. In a minute someone answered it. By now, it was useless to try going back to sleep. I was still tired, but my mind had started to work. Who was at the door? Maybe it was someone I really wanted to see. So I struggled out of bed to wash, shave and dress.

With waking, a flood of things to do, and people to see came back. It didn't seem impossible, as it had the night before, but the week-end was going to be heavy. I really should have got up at seven when the first call came. The file in my brief case had a list of people who must be seen, some of them miles away. They were depending on me to straighten out impossible messes. During the night, I had remembered an urgent call to be made, and scribbled it on a piece of paper. Yes, it was still there. I could have some breakfast and get on the road in an hour. I had come home on Thursday night this week-end, so that government offices would be open today. So many times things could have been cleared up with a couple of phone calls, but on Saturday the offices were closed. Mentally organizing a route that would get around to all the calls as conveniently as possible, I finished dressing and started downstairs for breakfast. Before I reached the bottom of the stairs, the telephone rang again. So I answered. It was an unemployment insurance delay. When the conversation was finished, I wrote down the information. I would wait awhile, because there would likely be more calls on unemployment insurance. It was a tragic situation this winter.

The next call came just as I was drinking my coffee. The lady couldn't get a rural mail box. "I'll see what I can find out and drop you a line," I promised. "I have to go now, there is someone at the door." After writing down her name and address, and the words "mail box" as a reminder, I went to the door. There were three men, members of a municipal council. They stamped the snow off their feet, took off their coats and sat down in the living room. They had three problem families in the township. These families can't get provincial welfare because they are entitled to federal assistance. But the federal money hasn't come through. The township clerk has all the details with him. There is another matter, too. The township has applied for a federal grant for winter employment but hasn't heard anything yet. If they are going to do the job this winter, they have to get started right away.

It was after nine, so Amelia Cole would be in the office in Ottawa. Placing a call, I gave her the unemployment insurance matter, the winter works application and the three pension cases. Find out about the winter works first, so I can get the council on its way; then as much of the other stuff as possible. It was fortunate I got right through. With luck I would have some answers in half an hour.

Marie had returned from a trip up town and was getting coffee for the councillors. As I went back to join them, the phone rang again. This time it was an old age pension problem.

"Mother just got a letter cutting her old age pension by $20.00," said the caller. "We think it's outrageous. She is very upset. She can't get out of the house in this weather. When can you come around to see her?"

A good question. "Sometime this weekend," I said. "That's all I can promise."

After two more calls, there was a report from Ottawa. It was good news. The winter works project had been approved, and there would be a letter in the mail today. The unemployment insurance problem had been straightened out. The three pension cases would be looked into. Thank God for a good secretary. The council took off in high spirits. I then called the unemployed man to tell him a cheque is on the way. Just hang on a few days longer.

It was now 11:00 o'clock. I decided to take a walk up town, get some fresh air, and see the postmaster about that mail box. It should only take a couple of minutes to get the story straight. The other calls could wait till I got back to Ottawa.

"I'll be heading North in half and hour," I told Marie. "Could you get me something to eat before I go?"

"I'll expect you back when you get here," she concluded from experience, "and I'll have something ready."

Stepping out into the bracing winter air, the weight seemed to lift a bit. I had accomplished quite a lot this morning. And with luck, the pressing matters could be cleared up this afternoon and evening.

"Well, you're sure an early bird," a voice broke in on my thought. It was one of the neighbours. "I wish I had a nice soft job like that — heading up town near noon. I have already done a day's work."

"I'll bet you have." There was no use trying to explain. He was partly kidding anyway, so I just kept walking.

It was about 1:30 in the afternoon when I got away. Driving in a rural constituency gives you time to think. Today I wondered again just what kind of a job I had got into. I had never expected to do social work, but that is exactly what it was. Sometimes it got me down. So many people just dropped their problems in my lap and said, "I'll leave it with you." Then after I did my best, they weren't satisfied.

There were several pleasant calls to make. People who appreciated my help. A couple celebrating their 50th wedding anniversary. Good news for an anxious mother whose son is in

106

penitentiary. I shared their pleasure in a leisurely atmosphere.

It was almost dark when I made the last call of the day. The house, if it could be called that, was perched on bare rock, beside a country road. Obviously hammered together out of rough lumber, it was small, unpainted and warped. One broken windowpane was covered over with cardboard. Everything about the place was barren, not a shrub, not a tree, not even a pathway to the door. My knock was answered by a thin little woman with stringy hair and a plain, weary face. I felt sorry for her.

As I went in there was a rustle and the squeak of bed springs as children disappeared into home-made bunk beds at one side of the building. Otherwise it was all one room. The furnishings consisted of a wooden table, a sink in one corner, a wood stove and several orange crates serving as chairs. Dominating the room was a television set, raised on a box and turned up loud. A man with a red face and an enormous belly sat on one of the orange crates watching the set. He didn't stir. The woman went over and turned down the volume, and he looked angry. However, when she told him who had come, he struggled to his feet.

"We're getting a raw deal from the welfare," he said, without waiting for any formalities. "You will have to straighten them out."

"What is the trouble?"

"We're not married, you know," he argued, "and they're always giving us trouble."

"You said in your letter you had financial problems," I said. "What are they?"

"The payment on the television is due and we can't pay it," the woman broke in. "It's only $15.00, but they are going to take it away if we don't pay this week."

I had a surge of impatience. It wasn't a Member's job to go around worrying about repossession of household goods. And nobody was going to give them help to keep a TV when they didn't even have a chair in the place. I said so. But they said the set meant a lot to the children, and the woman got her only pleasure in life from it. They seemed to get along well, as they sat there telling their troubles. I felt some compassion. This family was struggling against the world. And for lack of $15.00 they would lose what little they had. It occured to me that I had spent that much on an evening out. So I decided to give them the money. It was a waste of time to write to social agencies, and I might just as well get the problem off my hands right now. I would break my standing rule just this once.

"I think I can help you myself," I finally said, "but you must not tell anyone. I would be hounded to death."

They nodded in understanding. So I reached into my wallet and took out $15.00.

"Give it to me," she said, suddenly grabbing the money. "He will just drink it away."

"Damn you," he shouted, "if you weren't so miserable, I wouldn't drink at all."

"You're nothing but a lazy bum," she shouted back, "I don't know why I live with you."

"I know why," he yelled. "Nobody else will have you. No wonder your husband left you. If I was smart, I'd leave too."

"Go ahead, and good riddance," she yelled back. "At least the children wouldn't have a drunk stumbling in every night." The little shack was suddenly filled with hatred and abuse. They seemed to forget their visitor as the exchange became violent. For my part, I bade them a quick good-bye and got out, wondering faintly what would happen to my money.

Next morning found me visiting the lady with the pension problem.

"I just can't understand it," she said. "I have nothing coming in at all. But I received this letter saying that my old age supplement is being cut by $20.00 a month. How can they do that? It's all I have to live on." She had the official letter. The income tax office had reported interest of $122.35 which was not shown on her application. They would have to reduce her allowance by $10.00 per month, and also recover an overpayment by a further reduction of $10.00.

"They say you have interest coming in," I said to her. "Do you have any bonds or bank account or anything like that?"

"Just enough for my funeral and last expenses", she said.

"About how much, if you don't mind telling me?"

"A little over $2000."

Doing some quick mental calculations, I began to see the light. "May I see your bank book?" I asked.

She went and got it, and there was the answer. Two items of

interest the previous year totalling $122.35, about ten dollars a month.

"You didn't report this interest?" I asked.

"I honestly never thought of it," said the astonished lady. "I never drew it out, so I didn't get it. I wonder how they found out."

"The bank has to report interest earnings to the income tax office," said her Member, who had been through it before, "and the income tax office reports to Old Age Security."

"Well, I guess I made a mistake, all right," said the disappointed woman. "I will just have to get along some way. If they are that careful about my little bit, I guess they watch the big boys even closer."

"I guess so," I replied, opening the door. But I couldn't really believe it.

One of the great tragedies of social welfare systems is overpayment. Through ignorance or carelessness, an applicant is awarded a larger monthly payment than he or she is entitled to receive. Then one day it has to be paid back.

This double reduction taxes a pensioner's budget to the breaking point. It is one of the inevitable cruelties of a means test for welfare assistance.

Late Saturday afternoon, I finally got away to make two calls I had been putting off. They turned out just as unpleasant as I had expected. The first call was on a veteran who wanted a disability pension. Time and again the medical boards insisted that his condition had nothing to do with army service 25 years before. It was a normal aging process. But I had talked the board into one more hearing. Even the man's own doctor couldn't support his case. The poor fellow thought everyone was against him. He took out his annoyance on his caller, and I eventually got up and left.

I didn't look forward much to the second call either. This man wanted a government job which was open in his area. He wanted his Member to recommend him. Something stuck in that Member's mind. Just a little thing, maybe, but significant. A couple of weeks earlier when I answered the telephone, the operator said she had a collect call.

"I'm sorry," I had explained, "but I am not expecting a call from such a person. In any case, I do not accept collect calls."

"It's an urgent constituency matter," the caller had cut in. "When he hears about it he'll be glad to pay the charges."

"All right," I said, "I'll accept the call."

Then this fellow had asked for the position and spent 10 minutes explaining how well qualified he was.

"If he can swindle me like that," I thought as I hung up, "what a terrific job he could do on the public."

And I decided that I wouldn't send a letter of reference, even an evasive one. Local enquiries had confirmed my suspicions. However, the man had become a nuisance, and finally extracted the promise of a visit. So I had to break the bad news. Chiselling comes so naturally to this kind of person that he feels no self reproach. Nor did he now.

"You'll be sorry when this gets around," he warned. "You'll not get another vote around here if you won't give me a recommend."

"Several people told me I'd never get another vote if I did," replied his Member, "so it adds up about even."

I was pretty sure of my ground, but it was still unpleasant. The door closed on a torrent of abuse. It was well after dark as I drove off, hungry and depressed.

The roads in this area are open all winter, but there are times, on stormy nights, when they fill in with drifting snow. This was one of those nights. The wind was whipping snow up against the windshield, blowing in drifts across the single track road. Little gusts of wind were seeping through the cracks in doors and windows, and in spite of the full blast of the heater my ankles and lower legs were cold. The last call had been an unpleasant experience. Now I was headed for Parry Sound. It was too late to get home.

It was nearly 7:30 and dark. Hunger pangs were beginning to bother me. The wheel tracks ahead got fainter and fainter, and suddenly a small hill loomed from the darkness. My speed was too slow. Part way up the hill the wheels started spinning, and the car stopped. The only thing to do was to back down, and get a better run at it. Damn! The back wheels were off the road, and the car would not move. I sat there for a minute. How far ahead is the main highway? It is hard to know, exactly. How far back was that last house? A couple of miles, anyway. Well I might as well start walking. The best gamble was to go ahead. There may be something or someone nearby.

When I opened the car door, the fierceness of the cold became obvious. It must have gone down ten degrees in the last half hour.

110

My feet were wet from melted snow and they quickly chilled. The cold wind whipping around my face, under my coat and through my clothes caused me to lean forward and turn sideways against it.

"What in hell am I doing away out here anyway," I thought to myself. "Just a year ago, I was actually out busting my guts asking for this, spending my hard-earned money on advertising, posters, social evenings, meetings and heaven knows what else to get re-elected to Parliament."

Suddenly, a light appeared ahead. Closer up there was a small house. It looked very much like the one occupied by that miserable bastard five miles back. "Probably they have a vicious dog at the front door, half buried in the snow," I mumbled to myself. "They don't seem to have anything to tow me out with. They will probably not answer the door, or if they do, they will be surly and miserable."

That's the way it had been this afternoon. But there was no other light visible, and at least they might have a telephone. So I knocked.

The door swung open. A beautiful blast of warm air swept out. I could see someone putting wood on the fire, and the place was bright.

"Why, it's Mr. Aiken," exclaimed the lady at the door. "What on earth are you doing here at this time of the night?"

"Well, my car ran off the road just over the hill, and I can't get it moving. If I could just make a phone call, maybe somebody could come and pull me out."

"No need to phone anybody. My goodness, the boys will get you out in no time," she said. "Henry, it's our MP and he is stuck in the ditch."

She caught me by the sleeve as I stood there.

"Come on in out of the cold," she said. "You look half frozen."

"I guess I am."

Henry appeared from another room. They both looked familiar. My overcoat came off, my hands warmed over the fire, and the chill began to disappear. A cup of hot tea suddenly appeared, with some Christmas cake on the saucer. The first gulp of tea brought a warm feeling throughout my whole body, almost as if it were alcohol. A couple of husky-looking boys arrived, and then a young girl; all called in to meet the visiting dignitary. You would almost think it was a state visit, rather than an accidental stumble to the door.

"It is really an honour to have you in our home," she said. "We have seen you on television, and at meetings, and Henry drives for you on election day. You spoke to us once at the arena just before Christmas, but I don't suppose you remember. There were so many people around."

"You are both very familiar," I recalled. "I think I saw you at the fall fair in September."

"That's right, I had almost forgotten. Isn't that wonderful, Henry. He remembers meeting us at the Fair."

She went on about an elderly neighbour I had helped, an aunt and uncle to whom I had sent 50th wedding anniversary messages and other pleasant matters. The pangs of regret, the cold walk through the snow, the disagreeable encounters this afternoon, all began to fade into obscurity. I was here among friends I hardly knew five minutes ago. I began to think maybe it was worth-while winning that election after all. How many others were there along this road, in this township, who feel the same way? And here I was fifty miles from home. The car — I had almost forgotten it.

"If Henry and the boys can give me a hand," I said, "we should be able to get the car out and up the hill."

"You are not going out into that cold again," she insisted. "You just sit right there and warm up, and we will have it out in no time. There are chains on the half-ton for this road."

The men set off into the cold and darkness. The warmth had come back into my hands, feet, ears and body, and into my heart too. The friendly woman chattered away until soon we heard the sound of two motors roaring through the ruts and up to the door. She had given me some beef stew, warmed up from supper, another cup of tea, and a piece of pumpkin pie. There is nothing like a warm meal on a cold night.

As I drove off, it seemed incredible that my spirits had gone so low, and then risen so high. But looking back I realized that this had happened before. The good part generally came with meeting people in their own homes. If a riding is properly represented, I thought, the Member should be able to knock on any door and be greeted by name. I determined to keep trying, even with the hard cases. Maybe my efforts were appreciated after all.

112

There is good news for the constituency man, the social worker. He is doing what the people expect him to do. A recent poll asked Canadians to list the principal duties of an MP as they understand them. No hint whatever was given as to the type of answer expected. No sample replies nor choices were offered. And over half said, in one way or another, that looking after the problems of his constituents should be a Member's first priority. This was far ahead of any other suggestion. And very few Members who give it first priority are defeated.

THE PARTY MAN

To be part of the new government was exhilarating. It was almost like standing beside the turbine at a generating station. We could feel power surging outward from this central point to feed the boundless needs beyond. The engineer in charge, full of confidence, in full control of the men and machines around him, exuded a sense of excitement to his crew. Power in my hands; power in your hands; power received from the people, now directed back to them. That message needed no words; it was there, all-pervading, yet unspoken.

The focus of power turned first to the aged, languishing half forgotten in their retirement from bringing the country to its affluence. "How much should the old age pension be raised?" was the first question before the caucus of Progressive Conservative Members in 1957. It was a touchy subject. March, April and May had seen the "six buck boys" ridiculed to defeat. With the pension at $40.00, Finance Minister Walter Harris had put through an increase of 15 per cent, which came to $6.00. Conservative Leader John Diefenbaker had scorned this miserly attitude, and ended up on June 10th winner and Prime Minister. The new government would deliver on its promise to be more generous. But how much?

Some Member suggested the pension be raised to $50.00. "Would you like to be called the four-buck boys?" asked the new Prime Minister, and they allowed they wouldn't. A five-dollar increase, while a nice round figure, would leave the pension at $51.00, not a nice round figure. Opinion hovered around $55.00 and finally settled there.

"We never vote on these things," pointed out the chairman of caucus to the new Members. "However, I think we have a concensus."

But some of the Members were worried. "You can't increase

114

old age pensions without looking after the veterans, the blind and the disabled," someone said. "That's right," acknowledged the Prime Minister, "we will look after them as well."

Attention then turned to the economy. A tight money policy had brought things in Canada to a grinding halt. The general view was that more building construction would get things moving. It would use the large stocks of Canadian lumber and building supplies lying in the yards and warehouses, provide homes for the many young couples living with relatives or in rented rooms, and increase employment in country and city.

"A good suggestion," said the Prime Minister, writing it down.

The ideas poured out. Prairie farmers needed advances of cash on their crops, and farmers across the country wanted some price stabilization. The Atlantic provinces need financial help. The northern territories needed development funds.

And everything was favourable to the leadership. The sense of power and direction built up in the Members as they tackled the affairs of state. When caucus adjourned they were elated about all the problems they had solved. "Don't get too excited about it," cautioned the cynics, "we didn't settle anything. The cabinet makes the final decisions."

But this time they were wrong. That brief, eventful parliament immediately raised the old age pension to $55.00. Veterans, blind and disabled persons also got a similar increase. The government proposed a massive increase for home construction, and the money was quickly voted. Advance payments for prairie grain, farm price stabilization, and an increase in tax sharing with the Atlantic provinces quickly followed. One by one, caucus members saw their own grand proposals implemented. Even the old-timers were impressed; but still not completely.

"They probably had this all settled before caucus," said one, "we were just steered into approving."

On that score he may have been right. But the taste of power brought unity to those who indulged.

Every Wednesday morning when parliament is in session, the Members of each party march resolutely to caucus, determined to achieve unity. The wisdom of the ages, absorbed since childhood through legend and story, motivates their deliberations.

Aesop, purveyor of human truth through fables, first recorded the facts on unity 2,500 years ago.

"Union gives strength," he pronounced in *The Bundle of Sticks.* The adage has been repeated throughout history. It gave birth to the American union of states. "By uniting we stand, by dividing we fall," was the Liberty Song.

George Washington and Winston Churchill added their historic words. The truth of the principle is undeniable.

The party system in western democracy provides opposing positions on any matter. Some people believe that is enough. Internal division within the parties merely complicates things. That is certainly the view of party leaders. They prefer the strength of unity and the image of firm leadership. The leader's prayer for each caucus is to have full support for his decisions. Lacking it when caucus begins, he must convince the doubters and mute the critics. For the most part, he succeeds. "Blest be the tie that binds," murmurs the leader, as he searches for it continually. And the prospect of power is the most binding tie for Members.

But it's not just power. Party members back home and the public in general give the leader an assist. Party members have more interest in the party and the issues than they have in the Member himself. Therefore they become annoyed if the Member thinks he knows more than his party. Other voters have elected the Member as a means of putting his party into power. And while they berate backbenchers for lack of independence, they won't vote for those who get too independent. The pressure for unity comes from outside as well as inside.

So we are talking now about the things that hold Members to their party. Most of the pressure takes place in the caucus, the weekly meeting of the Members. It would be easier to write about caucus if I hadn't belonged to one. For caucuses are private. But there is a point in time when everything becomes history, and the privacy of caucus ends. That time has never been defined. John Diefenbaker, defender of tradition, disclosed in 1972 his caucus activities of 28 years earlier. Other caucus debates have been revealed in about 28 minutes. The time of disclosure seems to be left to the individual. So here goes.

For the first five years, Diefenbaker kept his caucus firmly under control. But when secrets began to leak out, he took it less and less into his confidence. The time of caucus became occupied with beef sessions. Having over 200 of the 265 Members, a few protest votes would never have hurt. But they were simply not allowed. The leader wanted unity, and unity he got. For now he was master of the House, made so by overwhelming public acclaim. The massive majority backed up its ministry with applause and cheering in the Chamber. There was so little external division that when Raymond Rogers wrote an article in Saturday Night in April 1961 entitled "Crossing the Tory Party Lines?" he had to use a question mark.

Oh, a few people came close to breaking out. In January 1960 Ed Nasserden got hot about the support price structure for eggs and hogs. After raising the matter with the minister and in caucus without result, he really hit it in a speech.

"It is a most retrograde step," he proclaimed. "The arguments used are unworthy of an informed ministry. It will drive the small producer out of business, encourage the speculator to manipulate prices and bring disorderly supply and marketing." But he stopped short of casting a dissenting vote.

A month later, Charlie Van Horne let loose a blast against the government over unemployment. But he didn't disturb the harmony in a vote. Next year, Ernie Broome took a hard line against a pipeline bill being sponsored by his colleague, Eldon Woolliams. He declared he would vote against it. The debate came to the Prime Minister's attention and he frowned. He was not pleased to have his Members quarrelling among themselves. The bill passed without a recorded vote.

I was another. On one occasion Diefenbaker was particularly annoyed over an appeal from the acting chairman, Ted Rea. He blamed him for a bad decision, and was making it clear in the lobby. Everyone was standing around agreeing. I though he was being unfair.

"I think he was perfectly right," said I, during a pause in the abuse.

The reaction was violent. Not only contradicted, he thought I was going to break ranks.

"Get in there and vote with your party," commanded the Prime Minister, eyes flashing and finger pointing. I did — that time.

After the 1962 election, when the government was nearly defeated, the pattern was the same. But the reason was different. The invincibility of the leader was no longer beyond question. His hold over his followers had weakened. But now it was a matter of

117

survival. The party had to stand together, or go down. It could not afford to lose a single vote. And no Member wanted to be on the wrong side in case of defeat. Even in the crucial vote on nuclear arms on February 5th, 1963, when many did not agree, two abstained, but no Conservative voted against the government.

Irresistible with a majority, compelling with a minority, Diefenbaker as Prime Minister had few outbreaks of public discord.

It came close once, in an emotional caucus held on February 6th, 1963. Into that meeting went a group of rebellious men, bent on either changing the leader's mind about his attitude to the Americans, and to nuclear arms, or resigning. Out of that meeting came a mollified and fighting group, ready to face an election. How did he do it? His grasp of the psychology and emotions of his followers was unique. And he used everything he knew. Unity was built on an insecure foundation, however, and soon collapsed.

Before concluding that absence of dissenting voices was due to heavy-handed discipline by John Diefenbaker, you have to look at the situation under his successor. Lester Pearson was entirely different in temperament, background and approach. He had practically no discipline in the party, and things were almost a shambles. His first parliament from May 1963 to June 1965 saw the most party splits in decades. There was internal division in 51 of the 124 recorded votes. 64 Members broke with their party, 16 of them on 5 or more occasions. Quite a record! But it wasn't Lester Pearson's Liberals who broke. Only 3 of his 128 Members ever recorded a dissenting vote. Government ranks sat laughing and scoffing as opposition parties divided time and again. Although it wasn't easy for a lot of government supporters, their duty was clear. The price of survival was constant loyalty to party and leader. "On several occasions I had to vote against my conscience," says Pauline Jewett looking back on this period, "and those times I felt I had no character at all. But I could see no alternative."

The Conservatives who for six years had stood solid as a rock, now split on several issues. Survival as the party in power was no longer at stake. The leader had no offices to give or withhold. A lot of the issues were emotional and moral, and natural divisions in party membership surfaced. The Social Credit and New Democratic parties also indulged themselves in extensive division, sometimes to prevent defeat of the government.

But occasionally the instinct for unity is overcome by total opposition to the leader's opinion. Then he must maintain the peace. Both Diefenbaker and Pearson had to back down at least once. For the former it came in the spring of 1965, on the opting-out formula in federal provincial programs. The formula was constructed specially for Quebec. He was absolutely opposed to special arrangements for one province. He announced his intention of opposing it. But this raised two problems. Four Conservative premiers had already approved. Opposition at the federal level would repudiate them. Also it would place the party in an anti-Quebec position, and that was bad enough already. Even his loyalists balked. After trying several manoeuvres over a period of time, he found caucus a stone wall. He then reversed his position and the bill went through quietly.

Pearson's trouble was a year later, in February, 1966. It occurred in the case of George Victor Spencer, a former civil servant accused of spying. Sick to death of enquiries and royal commissions into scandal, Pearson refused to set up another enquiry in which to flounder. But his followers saw greater dangers in refusing; allegations of a cover-up. When rumour of an opposition motion got around, the caucus acted. If a vote were forced, came the verdict, many would have to support an enquiry or stay away. The government could easily be defeated. Pearson backed down, and personally announced an enquiry.

If a leader really tries, a determined caucus can be beaten without backing down, and without public discord. On Wednesday, April 20th, 1966, word got around that Flora MacDonald had been fired from the staff at Progressive Conservative headquarters. It was stunning news to everyone, as she had been consistent and impartial through several years of crisis. Caucus was going to get someone for that. But the leader was not present, and everyone else was vague about responsibility. The following Wednesday saw a show-down looming. But when Members arrived for caucus they found it had been cancelled. By the next week, it was all over and Flora had departed.

When Pierre Trudeau was elected as Prime Minister, he had some changes to make. He was repelled by the looseness of

Pearson's management of cabinet and caucus. Elected with a solid mandate, he let it be known, publicly and privately, that things would tighten up. He would not fumble around with people who operate on emotion rather than modern administrative techniques. And there were going to be no leaks, or dire consequences would follow. He put caucus in its place by building up a counter-organization in his office, which soon became the source of political advice. Legislative programs began to appear without any hint to caucus.

As complaints developed and caucus became a nuisance, systems were developed to cut down the flack. An agenda, prepared in advance, was strictly followed. This effectively cut off general complaints and loose discussion of policy matters and party direction. More caucus committees were set up, which directed Members' attention to specific bills rather than general matters. Party members no longer felt themselves an effective part of the policy process. The inducement for a team spirit vanished.

"The backbencher is now effectively insulated from power," said Raymond Rock as he left the Liberal party in 1972. And it showed in the October election.

Robert Stanfield's way with caucus is different. Taking over a badly divided party in 1967, he spend his first years bringing it together into an effective and united force. In this he succeeded through patient discussion and reason. But when pushed too far, he occasionally reacts with anger and remarkable firmness. He once bluntly told the group which had got into difficulty over a bilingualism vote that they should have foreseen the result. "Anyone who thought otherwise," he admonished, "doesn't have two pieces of brain to rub together." Sometimes he goes further, and lets loose some of the saltiness of his Maritime background.

But he is not too disturbed at occasional failure to achieve a united front, if divergent beliefs are honestly and firmly held. Therein lies his strength.

Tommy Douglas managed to keep reasonable discipline in the New Democrats' caucus. David Lewis is positive with his Members, and they respect him. Not too much leaks out. Real Caouette has firm control of the Social Credit group. Their strength is in small numbers.

Outside observers sometimes find it difficult to understand

how successful business men — lawyers, managers, farmers, merchants, university professors, engineers, doctors and teachers — can check their independence at the door when they go to caucus. How can they go along with a decision they do not approve? What makes unity so important? If they knew how Alonzo Martin handled it perhaps they would understand it better. A member of the Liberal caucus early in 1969 when legal abortion was proposed, Martin believed the proposal wrong. So did most of his constituents. He was opposed to any change in the law.

"This is very difficult for me," he said when he got the floor. "I believe there are no grounds for taking human life, and so do most of my constituents."

Encouraged by scattered applause, he went on. "Abortion is contrary to the laws of God and nature. A foetus is a human being, entitled to be brought into the world."

There was no doubt a lot of Members agreed with him. As he sat down, he felt better for saying it. The Prime Minister, in fact, smiled in appreciation of his problem. But he said nothing.

"Right now it would be a lot easier if we were Creditistes," he muttered to his neighbour. "They have come out as a party against any changes."

"Well, if you want to belong to a small regional party, go ahead," replied the other. "But they don't feel the power of being a national party in government."

That was true, Martin sat thinking. But in such a big party as this, surely there is room for a few dissenters. To speak out publicly against abortion would bring quiet words of praise from many sources. But where would it lead politically? Not very far. Trudeau was elected at the national convention, and is responsible to the party, not to me. And he just led us to a majority victory. The party members wouldn't want me to oppose him now. Loyalty is important. I might not even get the next convention.

"Do you think I could talk to the PM privately and tell him my position?" he wondered aloud. "Maybe he would understand if I went against the party just this once."

"He knows your position already," replied the friend. "He's just interested in your vote now. It's his pet project. He won't change his mind."

"But if I were the only one, it wouldn't really be a revolt."

"Gordon Sullivan has already stated he will vote against the abortion part," replied his counsellor. "You might make it a revolt."

That's right, Martin thought. Unless I really decide to desert, the PM shouldn't know I have disloyal thoughts. Any chances for a cabinet job would end. Anyway, I want to get on that United Nations delegation this fall. Causing trouble would end that too. Best to keep quiet for the moment.

The Prime Minister got up and left for another appointment. It might be a little easier to talk now. "Maybe these fellows who feel so strong could speak against the abortion part, and then vote for the whole bill," suggested a helpful Member. "There are plenty of good things in it."

"Where will that leave them if the Creditistes move to strike out the abortion clause?" asked another. "Our fellows could either vote with the Creditistes, the way they talked; or reverse themselves publicly." Not much of a choice.

"Don't forget there is a medical committee," said Justice Minister John Turner. "They will watch things pretty closely."

That helps, thought Martin. Maybe the change is not so bad after all. I'll have to think about this before making a foolish move.

"Are we all agreed then?" the voice of the caucus chairman broke in on his thoughts. "We will stand together and support the whole bill."

A murmur of assent went round the room. Some sat silent. Martin had to speak now if he was ever going to. The majority is in favour, he thought, and they rule in a democracy. I expressed myself strongly, so my conscience is clear. But I have been overruled. Maybe I should just say something, though, to protect my position. But as he rose to speak, he found the caucus was over.

Alonzo Martin is a pseudonym. But the rest of the story is as true as a second-hand story can be. It is typical of dozens of other situations.

Not everybody agrees that political parties are a good thing. "Party is the madness of many, for the gain of the few," wrote Jonathan Swift over 250 years ago. "The one pervading evil of democracy is the tyranny of that party that succeeds by force or fraud in carrying elections," wrote Lord Acton 75 years ago.

"Political parties are the curse of today's parliaments," wrote Canadian journalist Harold Greer in 1972.

In spite of adverse opinion for 250 years, the party system survives, strong and overpowering as ever. So it looks fairly permanent as part of western democracy. In Canada, there is a special need. The great diversity in regions, people, resources and living conditions make necessary a national outlook on basic problems. Parties force a national consensus rather than a series of regional approaches.

Since the strength of party is unity, the pressure for unity will remain.

Since leaders derive their power from loyalty, they will continue to reward it.

And since party gives the Member his vehicle to success, he must surrender some independence in return. Just how much he surrenders depends upon the individual. We will look at that next.

THE DISSENTERS

"Not Me, You Don't"

In spite of all efforts to maintain unity, every party has a few who just won't fall into line. They are always arguing, doubting and dissenting — and then they prove their point by splitting the vote.

York North, for example, produces its own particular breed of politician. It's a standing legend around parliament hill that you have to be a millionaire businessman with an independent mind to get elected there. The facts aren't that far off.

C.A. "Tiny" Cathers filled the bill from 1957 to 1962. He was a big man, straightforward and never confused by other people's facts. He called himself a farmer, but he also had business interests and money. When he was chairman of the Banking and Commerce Committee, lawyer Paul Martin was trying to quote the rules to him. Cathers was not impressed.

"I don't know much about the rules," he said, "but by God that doesn't sound right to me."

Martin pointed out that he could force the chairman to follow proper procedures.

'No me, you don't,' said the Member for York North. And he didn't.

North York's Wallace McCutcheon didn't quite make it to the Commons, but he was appointed to the Senate. Well established in the business and financial world, he brought a no-nonsense attitude towards politics. He saw things as they were, and spoke them. It didn't get him very far, but he didn't care. He apparently told the leader privately late in 1964 that he ought to retire. Diefenbaker later complained that this caused a lot of harm.

"I never told anybody about it," responded McCutcheon. "I wonder who did." He always asked direct questions.

John Addison was elected for York North in 1962. An affluent young car dealer and investment executive, he didn't think too much of the system, either. But he was re-elected twice, maintaining his independence in the process. In December of 1967, he came face-to-face with reality. He had been complaining publicly and privately about the government's easy spending habits. Then they brought in a budget with tax increases, which hit business hard. Addison knew what would happen. Business would merely pass the increase on to the consumer, and set up another round of inflation.

On Monday, December 11th, the opposition moved non-confidence in John Addison's government. It regretted "that the government has proposed an increase in taxes to meet its extravagance, thus contributing to the inflationary pressure on the economy." Exactly what Addison had been saying.

The vote proceeded normally Monday night. After the opposition votes had been counted, clerk assistant Gordon Dubroy cast his eye around the House to see if there was anyone else. Up popped a figure on the government side. "Mr. Addison," he called out, as necks in the front bench craned to see what had gone wrong. Something was wrong, all right. A Member had looked at the words in the motion, not at the authors, and voted the way he believed. It was taking a chance in a minority position, but fortunately the government survived. Addison didn't.

"I've been sent to Coventry," he said later; and when the 1968 election rolled around, he wasn't running.

Going it alone is not always a bad thing. Leaders expect some spin-off. The loner may even become an asset if time proves him right, and he survives long enough. He can be quoted later to show that "we" were right.

Dissenters have an urge for power too, but it takes on a new twist. David MacDonald, himself no mean "trouble-maker" puts it this way: "Some people aspire to power through ginger groups. They feel power in challenging accepted opinion and changing it.

Whatever the reason, it's much easier to break ranks if it happens in other parties at the same time. Take the bilingualism issue, for example. In October 1968, the government introduced the Official Languages Act, under which federal government services would be provided in both English and French in bilingual areas of the country. Robert Stanfield decided that in principle he would support it. Then began the long pull to bring caucus in behind him. There were two forces working against him: personal beliefs and regional prejudice.

Quite a few Members believed personally that to expand bilingualism in Canada was merely to expand the conflict. Regionally, western Canada and areas of the east were opposed to any extension of the use of French, outside Quebec.

But Stanfield saw a broader picture. Patiently, week by week, he talked out the problems of national unity with the hard-liners. He won over those who were motivated by personal opinion. But those who believed their constituents were also opposed would not commit themselves. They argued back.

"You will lose the West with that attitude," they told him, "and you will gain nothing in Quebec."

As the day of reckoning arrived in May 1969, however, it looked as if his patience had paid off. The other parties, appreciating Stanfield's efforts, and hoping to display some national unity on the matter, would not insist on a recorded vote. This was a great break for the Conservatives, who would be saved the embarrassment of a public split. Those who objected could call out "on division" to indicate that there was opposition. The fight would be in committee.

But other forces were at work. When the big moment came, seven western Conservatives stood up rebelliously to force a recorded vote. When the vote came, the seven were joined by ten others including former leader John Diefenbaker. He, by his front bench position, led off the dissenting vote to the grim-faced embarrassment of the other party members.

Then came the payoff. Seeing the massive split across the Chamber, and noting that it was mostly West versus East, B.C. Liberal Doug Stewart gathered up his courage and voted against the bill too. He stood alone on the government side.

A Member who has spoken early, often and publicly on an issue before it becomes a test of loyalty has an easier time. Colleagues forgive and forget if he has made a hobby-horse of it over the years. Thus when a clause to ease abortions was put in the Criminal Code bill of 1969, Gordon Sullivan was forgiven for standing alone in his party to vote against it. For he had made his position against abortion quite clear from the beginning. It was a vote for himself rather than against the party.

The same bill brought out a number of other loners. Liberal

John Reid stood alone to support Creditiste Romuald Rodrigue, who wanted medical committee decisions to be unanimous. Reid also joined loner John Burton of the NDP to restrict abortion to cases where the mother's life is in danger. Both motions were defeated. Finally when Gilbert Rondeau moved to strike out all abortion changes, Reid and Ralph Stewart supported him. It was a lost cause, and they were in no real danger. But their views are on record, backed by a recorded vote.

Some people wonder how Gordon Fairweather lasts as Member for Fundy Royal. He has firm views on many subjects such as recognition of the French fact in Canadian life, abolition of capital punishment and social welfare needs. His opinions amount merely to finding an honest answer to the problem. The result seems to put him in the "left wing," wherever that is. Now, a dissenter is fairly safe if he agrees with the party in parliament, though that may be out of tune with riding. And he is safe if he disagrees with the parliamentary group, but has the feel of the riding. When he is in disagreement with both, trouble awaits; and it often awaits Gordon Fairweather.

"They have always grudgingly let me go along on those issues I care about," he says of his constituents. He also knows that his constituents are just a bit smarter than they get credit for. And they put a high value on honesty. "Though an honest answer was unpopular," he says of a grilling he once got on bilingualism, "I had to give it."

To know how much internal party division there really is, you have to look at the "free" votes. There has really only been one in the past decade. That was on capital punishment in 1967. The government released all its Members, including ministers, from party ties. It introduced a bill, then let the House do what it would, without any question of confidence involved. The Members then formed themselves into cross-party pressure groups. A small group of Conservatives joined with some Liberals and the NDP to spearhead the abolition of capital punishment. They were in the minority. By wheeling and dealing they were able to swing over enough Members to get approval of partial abolition. Murder of law enforcement officers would still bring the death penalty. When the revised bill came to a vote, 15 Conservatives, 81 Liberals and all NDP Members were in favour; 56 Conservatives, 23 Liberals (including cabinet ministers) and all Social Crediters were against. That tells quite a story. There was a somewhat similar vote on the same subject in May, 1973, with similar results. In the later vote, however, the cabinet members stood solid.

The hate literature bill of 1970 had a real conflict in principles, and a free vote would have been interesting. For years minority groups in Canada, particularly the Jewish community, had asked for protection from tracts which stir up racial or religious hatred. Previous governments had avoided legislation. To ban literature of any kind is to restrict freedom of speech and freedom of the press. Yet racial prejudice has no place in Canada and the bill, while weak, was a token effort.

Once the government decided to bring in a bill, the course was set for government supporters. No free vote was offered. It was then up to the opposition parties to respond. The Conservatives had to decide between freedom of speech and protection of minority groups. The party stood in favour of both. An opposition party, if in doubt, attacks. So Eldon Woolliams, justice critic, plunged in and moved to strike out the section prohibiting hate literature.

"Canada is a tolerant nation," he argued, "and we have no need for this kind of legislation."

But he reckoned without his friend and colleague, Lincoln Alexander.

"I'll not vote against any effort to reduce racial discrimination in Canada, no matter how weak," said Linc "and I will go it alone if I have to."

But he didn't have to. When the vote came, nine other Conservatives stood with him.

The move, however, put a hard decision before the NDP. They were caught between the same two basic principles. The bulk of their Members supported the government, but four split to vote for the Conservative amendment. And once again, division in the opposition encouraged a government dissenter to stand up alone. John Roberts risked ministerial frowns to support the Woolliams amendment. He didn't do it again, though. He was defeated in 1972.

Some people never bother going to caucus. "It's just a lot of yack," they say. Also, some are out of town or busy with something more urgent on caucus day, and don't get there. They may hear second-hand what was discussed, and what consensus was reached, or they may be too busy to enquire. Then one day a Member is interrupted in his office or in committee by the division bells ringing.

"What are we voting on? he asks when he gets to the lobby.

"That agriculture bill," says a colleague, "we're all going to vote for it."

"What?" says the new arrival, "I wanted to talk on that. I'm not going to support it."

"But it was agreed in caucus," says his informant, "we spent two hours on it."

"Well, I wasn't there, and there's no way I'm going to vote for that mess."

Then there is a mini-caucus for a few minutes in the lobby. But the new arrival doesn't get the drift of the reasoning, which seemed so clear in caucus. If he is strong-willed, he may just get up on the spur of the moment and cast a dissenting vote. It's called living dangerously.

Some dissenters, however, have made their position clear from the beginning. Caucus discussions have left them unmoved. So have all other pressures to conform. They are willing to accept any unpleasant results which follow. They will not be trained seals. Neither will they be rebels, for they seek to protect the party interest when their colleagues appear wrong. Here is a classic example.

In a small classroom at Collège Militaire Royal in St. Jean, Quebec, André Rény was conducting his immersion course in French for English-speaking Members of Parliament. It was supposed to be a full week of tuition with no English spoken, and without interruption. So there was just a flicker of annoyance when David MacDonald was called to the telephone. Rény was accustomed to the unpredicatable activities of the Members. Some weeks, only half of them showed up. One of these might suddenly leave. He could adjust to this, if only he had their undivided attention when they were present. But there were always these telephone calls from Ottawa. Well, there wasn't much he could do about it, so there was no point in getting excited.

David shortly came back into the classroom. "Il faut retourner à Ottawa," he reported. About to comment, Rény changed his mind. If MacDonald had to return to Ottawa, then he would go. It wouldn't be the first time a Member just up and left.

"I think the party is wrong to support that bill," David told me later as he packed up to leave. "I'm going to speak in caucus about it tomorrow morning."

"I agree in principle," I said, "but we asked the government to bring it in. How can we now vote against it?"

"We didn't ask them to bring in this bill," said David "I just got the details. It's much worse than I ever expected."

"But it's a lot better than the War Measures Act which we have now," I pointed out.

"That doesn't make it right," he replied. "Anyway I'm going to see what I can do."

"The vote should come around the end of the week," I commented as he left. "Let me know and I'll come back."

The government of Canada had proclaimed the War Measures Act in effect at 4:00 a.m. on October 16th, to deal with an apprehended insurrection in the province of Quebec. The action had seemed dangerous to a lot of people concerned about civil liberties, especially when it was followed by the arrest and imprisonment without trial of about 400 people. Worse, the government would give no undertaking how long it would hold on to these war-time powers, or what use would be made of them. Such arbitrary powers were tailor-made for anyone with autocratic tendencies, and Prime Minister Trudeau had already shown these.

But public opinion suddenly solidified on Saturday, October 17th with the assassination of FLQ hostage Pierre Laporte. Horror and outrage at the murder of Quebec's Minister of Labour stirred up Canadians to support the government in any action it took against the instigators. On Sunday night, the Prime Minister made a superb appearance on television, showing himself as cold, implacable and determined in his efforts to wipe out the FLQ, a blot on the Canadian landscape. It was his finest hour, and the people were with him.

Tommy Douglas, leader of the New Democratic Party, was caught in a trap. He had taken a strong stand against imposition of the War Measures Act. On the very day Laporte was murdered, but without knowledge of the fact, he made his position clear in Western Canada. But on Monday, when a vote was called to approve the imposition of war measures, Canadians were no longer concerned about the niceties of civil liberties. Those in Quebec were frightened and wanted protection. Those outside Quebec felt no threat to their liberties. They wanted that rebellion choked off by any means.

After the government undertook to bring in substitute legislation, all other parties and Members supported imposition of the war measures. But Douglas and 15 of his followers had refused. They were universally condemned, even by party members. It was probably his hardest decision and lowest hour.

On Wednesday, November 4th, after two weeks of severe buffeting by Canadians, Douglas and his party were anxious to display their patriotism. They would support the Public Order Act, 1970, which had been proposed Monday. Opposition Leader Robert Stanfield had also been under heavy criticism for holding back in the beginning. And having asked for substitute legislation and repeal of the War Measures Act, he could hardly refuse when he got it. The Creditistes had supported the government from the beginning.

Every Member was anxious to prove his determination in the face of violence. Every Member, that is, except one. Having returned to Ottawa from his French course on Tuesday, November 3rd, and having failed to convince caucus, David MacDonald made his own decision. The bill was wrong in principle, and dangerous in precedent. So he voted against strong national opinion, his own party's decision, and the undoubted views of his constituents. The bill got second reading that Wednesday afternoon on a vote of 196 in favour, 1 opposed. The single act restored the faith of a lot of Canadians in their political system. One voice spoke for those who still thought the government wrong. It requires some special kind of courage to stand alone against your party. But against the whole House is something else.

To Kay McPherson, watching from St. Paul's riding in Toronto it proved that independence is more valuable than party voting. She later ran as an independent candidate in 1972.

"When David MacDonald, the Conservative from the

Maritimes, broke party solidarity to vote against the War Measures Act," she later told a reporter, "his decision had more effect than anything else he's done."

When the bill finally came up for third reading, David had some more support. Gordon Fairweather and I stood with him, to disapproving silence in the ranks made worse by support from the New Democrats who switched back to their original position.

The moment of voting is a Member's solitary decision. The welfare of the country, the special needs of his constituency or his own conscience sometimes overcome the strong compulsion to vote with his colleagues. But not often.

Sir Arthur Sullivan put over the advantages of solid voting 100 years ago in the well known verse from H.M.S. Pinafore:

I always voted at my party's call
And I never thought of thinking for myself at all,
I thought so little they rewarded me,
By making me the ruler of the Queen's Navee.

The strange thing is that most everyone still believes him. There are enough examples to make it plausible. The public doesn't support a dissenting voter. He is a bad example of discipline. Those in authority prefer trained seals. The Members themselves see how things go. But fortunately, there are enough surprises when the vote is called to keep things uncertain. That's good for the system.

THE REBELS

"I've Had It"

Then there are those who find their party hopeless. They argue, vote the wrong way and wrestle with their conscience, but find it all a waste of time. They are just not in tune with leader and party. Eventually they either leave their party or are kicked out. These people I call rebels, and they are part of this story too. I have made a tally of those who rebelled during my time. I knew them all, because rebels are not easily overlooked. But that doesn't mean they look the part.

I have already mentioned in passing Jean François Pouliot. He didn't really do his rebelling bit when I was there, because he had been pushed off to the Senate two years earlier. In the Senate you don't rebel, you disagree. But I had read his name in the papers on and off for years, and had the picture of a loud-mouthed ruffian. Then one day in New York at the United Nations Assembly where he came as an observer, I met him. He was charming, well groomed, pleasant and soft-spoken; one of the kindest French gentleman I have ever met. Of average height, heavily built and developing a stoop with his advancing years, he was just a quiet old-timer shuffling around the Canadian mission. But I knew something of his story, and when I showed interest, he responded. Elected as an independent, he was later admitted to the Liberal caucus. But his uncompromising views on conscription, Quebec's heritage, Mackenzie King and Louis St. Laurent kept him constantly in hot water. His opinions were the same in caucus, in the House, and to the press. His words were direct, frank and uncompromising. He voted as he spoke.

"You don't have to shout to speak unpleasant truths," he told me.

Eventually he was expelled from the Liberal caucus. "On many occasions when I went into the lobby not one of my colleagues would speak to me," he said. "They would pretend not to see me and turn the other way. They were always furious with me over something."

Pouliot never intended to be unpleasant. He just said what he thought, and he had a critical mind. Even after expulsion from caucus, the government couldn't stand him in the Commons. So he was appointed to the Senate to bother them over there. I often found myself wondering if this was really the same person I had read about. Maybe he had mellowed with age. But one day the Canadian delegation saw the shades of his former self. As Pouliot was about to return to Ottawa, Howard Green, Leader of the delegation, asked him at the morning meeting if he would like to say something.

"Well, just a couple of words, Mr. Green," said the Senator deferentially. "I found these morning meetings poorly prepared and badly handled. The library is terrible, and just the chosen few like yourself get the despatches from Ottawa. The young people here are polite, but that's all. They really don't know what is going on. I only had one job to do, and you gave me no instructions. It was a silly thing, anyway. There is a complete lack of organization in the mission and a lot of time is wasted. You, Mr. Green, are responsible for all this as leader of the delegation. I am sorry I wasted my time coming here."

"Thank you, Senator," said the Minister of External Affairs with a weak smile. "I should have known better than to ask." Jean François Pouliot died July 6th, 1969, still saying what he thought.

The public doesn't seem to like rebels too much. Their general fate is defeat at the following election, or dropping out to avoid it. Keep this in mind as we go through the list.

Ross Thatcher was elected to the House in 1945 as a member of the CCF party. But by 1955 he became disillusioned with socialism, and joined the Liberals. He ran for re-election in Assiniboia in 1957 and was defeated by Hazen Argue of the CCF. He tried again in 1958 and this time ran third. He didn't let these rebukes discourage him. He became leader of the Saskatchewan Liberal party in 1959 and was elected to the assembly in 1960. By 1964 he was premier of the province. But in 1971 his government was defeated by the New Democrats. Though personally re-elected, he took it so hard he died exactly ten days later at the age of 54.

A strange sequel to the Thatcher story was provided by the man who twice defeated him in Assiniboia. Hazen Argue was parliamentary leader of the CCF - NDP group from 1958 to 1962. But after the New Democratic party was formed in 1960 he saw the party becoming dominated by labour. He followed the lead of Ross Thatcher and joined the Liberals. He squeaked in as a Liberal in 1962 by 353 votes. In 133 he was defeated. In 1965 he was defeated again. But if the electors didn't appreciate his switch, the Liberals did. He was appointed to the Senate in 1966.

The next two who left their party started out as ultra-loyalists. When Réal Caouette split from the Social Credit party in September, 1963, Gerard Girouard and Gerard Ouellet stayed with the leader, Robert Thompson. Gradually, however, the situation in the party became hopeless, as Caouette vied with Thompson in a constant game of one-upmanship. In April, 1964, Girouard announced that he was joining the Conservatives. "The Social Credit party has fallen to pieces on account of its internal quarrels and its hopeless strife," he explained.

Ouellet then stated that he found himself in the same position and was also joining the Conservatives. Both sat with the offical opposition until the House dissolved in September 1965 for a general election. Ouellet ran again in Rimouski as a Conservative and got the grand treatment reserved for rebels. He received 1,477 votes, running fourth, defeated by Liberal Guy Leblanc with 11,369 and beaten by both Creditiste and New Democrat candidates as well. Girouard ran in Hull. He was similarly creamed, coming fourth with 1,875 votes against Liberal Member Alexis Caron's 17,858. These were former sitting Members!

While the Conservatives gained two Members in 1964, they were in the process of losing two others. The idea of a Quebec lieutenant for the party leader had been strong among Quebec Members. Léon Balcer was the obvious man, and his recognition as such was pressed on Mr. Diefenbaker. But it was never granted. For this and other reasons, a deep breach developed between the leader and the Quebec Members. In January 1965 they had a meeting and expressed confidence in Balcer. They then requested a meeting of the party national executive to consider a leadership convention.

Dalton Camp, national president, called a meeting for Saturday, February 6th. But the leader, always fast with a manoeuvre, called caucus for Friday, the 5th, even though the House was in recess. Having majority support in caucus, it was intended to read Balcer out of the party, and to obtain a unanimous vote of confidence in the leader. This would make the executive easier to handle. A small but firm caucus group obstructed both purposes. After an all-day wrangle on Saturday, the national executive announced that no convention would be called. Balcer said no more. But Rémi Paul was finished. On February 18th, two days after the House resumed, he left the party.

"I regret that I must leave the ranks, not of the Conservative party, but of the Diefenbaker party," he announced. "As of this day I shall sit in this House as an independent Member."

Rémi Paul's action was a shock. He was a solid Member and had not said too much publicly. He had occupied the Speaker's chair on many occasions in the 25th parliament as deputy chairman of committees. In the face of an election, efforts were made to prevent any futher defection. But relations between Balcer and Diefenbaker were completely torn. Finally, Balcer made it official on April 5th, 1965 and announced his decision to sit as an independent. Neither Paul nor Balcer sought re-election to parliament. Paul ran successfully in 1966 for the Quebec Assembly as a member of the Union Nationale, and became Speaker. Balcer ran as a Liberal and was defeated.

Though his party is composed entirely of Quebec Members, and their interests are in that province, Réal Caouette is a staunch Canadian. He continually promotes a better deal for Quebec, but always within the concept of confederation. But Gilles Grégoire, his deputy, became convinced in 1966 that Quebec had to reach its destiny alone. That summer he formed a separatist party in Quebec, the Ralliement National, and became its leader. Grégoire was promptly barred from the Creditiste caucus. On August 29th he asked to be seated as an independent. But it was not an angry separation. "Whenever the discussion will turn to social credit," he avowed, "I will always be ready to co-operate with my former leader and colleagues, for whom I still have the highest regard."

Grégoire was given a seat on the government side of the House, and found himself in contact with Ralph Cowan, a strong-minded Liberal, who looked and acted like a rebel. Between them, they began to upset the House by procedural tactics and long speeches. But they were in no way compatible. Cowan was just as strong against separatism as Grégoire was for it. The Liberals treated the subject very cautiously. But Cowan was not one to tread gently. When Grégoire was making his violent independence speeches, Cowan heckled loudly from a few seats away. His colleagues wished he would keep quiet. Finally, Grégoire challenged Cowan to go into Quebec and repeat his remarks there. Cowan promptly accepted. In 1967 the two of them debated Quebec's future in the high schools and universities of that province.

This activity literally drove the Liberal heirarchy up the wall. Cowan wasn't just against separatism. He felt Qubec was already getting more than it deserved. He had facts and figures to prove it. He tramped heavy-footed over Quebec sensitivities and he did it as a Liberal. Cabinet ministers had to run around for months patching up the damage.

Cowan had already made himself unpopular in March 1966 when he blocked a plan to continue the debate on capital punishment. On the 30th day of that month he also led an attack on minister George McIlraith which almost prevented approval of estimates. He constantly occupied caucus time with dissenting views. And after the separatism debates he got off on broadcasting policies. From second reading of the broadcasting bill to third reading three months later, Cowan spoke 22 times and Grégoire 21. Cowan moved two formal amendments and Grégoire four. On one occasion, Cowan felt it necessary to explain his pure Liberal background. "I consider myself a Liberal. Some people call me a Liberal of the Liberals," he said in the House, "I am anxious to find out whether this is Liberal doctrine. In my opinion it is not."

When Judy LaMarsh moved third reading in February 1968, Ralph Cowan moved a stalling amendment. He found support with the Conservatives and Grégoire. The amendment was defeated, but his colleagues were boiling about his defiance and the time lost. Two weeks later he was at it again. Defeated on a tax bill, the government was trying to pull itself together by a confidence vote. During the debate, Grégoire undertook to support the government if they would agree to his demands. He put them in the form of an outrageous amendment on February 23rd. Cowan seconded the amendment without even reading it. The motion was ruled out of order.

Having survived the vote of confidence, the government then substituted another tax bill. When it came to a vote, Cowan voted against it. That was the last straw. He was expelled from caucus. When the nomination for High Park was held for the 1968 election, he was defeated as Liberal candidate by Walter Deakon. So he ran as an independent liberal. He came fourth, a popular position for rebels. To Deakon's 16,260 votes, Cowan got 2,895. He didn't run for parliament again. As for Grégoire, his separatist group was absorbed in a confederation of separatists and he lost the leadership. He didn't run again either.

Now we come to the success story. There is always one. Horace (Bud) Olson was a long-time Social Credit supporter. First elected in 1957, he was defeated in 1958 but re-elected in 1963 and 1965. Part of the small western group, he stayed quietly loyal to Robert Thompson through all the trouble with Caouette. But in the 1965 election, Thompson's Quebec supporters were defeated, and he was left with only 5 Members in the House. He resigned as national leader to permit reorganization. Feeling the winds of change, Olson left his party in September 1967 and joined the Liberals. He was a prize possession right then. The Liberals only had one Member from all three prairie provinces, and that was Minister Roger Teillet from Manitoba. Olson not only doubled the prairie contingent, he was an authentic farmer. In the general election of 1968, nine prairie Members were elected. All were new and none were farmers. Except Olson. So he stepped neatly into the obvious post of Minister of Agriculture and held it honourably during the entire 28th parliament. But he could not resist the Conservative sweep of Alberta in 1972, and was defeated.

The loyalist who spent six years condemning and contriving against rebels in the Conservative party became one himself in 1968. Gordon Churchill found absolute loyalty easy with Diefenbaker. While they occasionally disagreed on tactics, their general philosophy was identical. As House Leader and chief lieutenant, Churchill knew instinctively how to react to any situation. Politics is total war, and the Grits are the enemy. Compromise is capitulation. Every proposal from the other side is a trick. He found the going harder with Stanfield, who had a somewhat different approach. And the break wasn't long in coming.

On February 19th, 1968, just three months after Robert Stanfield took his seat as Leader of the Opposition, the government lost the vote on a tax bill 82 to 84. By constitutional practise, Lester Pearson should have submitted his resignation as Prime Minister. But he didn't. Instead he treated the two-vote defeat as an accident. The bill had passed previous stages, including a vote on second reading. Almost 100 Members on both sides had been absent. He introduced a motion of confidence in the government to wipe out the tax bill failure.

Gordon Churchill and a number of Conservatives proposed that the confidence motion be filibustered indefinitely until the government collapsed. Having introduced the motion, the government had put its own status in question. No other business could be done until that was settled. Pearson had submitted his resignation as party leader, and a new convention had been called for April 4th. If an election could be forced immediately, the Liberals might be in a mess.

There were strong arguments against this strategy. Party members and public expected more from the new Conservative leader than filibuster. The election could be deferred until after the Liberal convention and the new leader would swing in on all the publicity. But the critical factor was not partisan. At that very moment, there was an economic crisis. The dollar was under attack and Canadian financial stability was in question. A prolonged deadlock in parliament, cutting off public funds, and the stagnancy of an election period could severely damage confidence in Canada. Himself an economist, Stanfield consulted independent experts, who confirmd that a filibuster strong enough to collapse the government, could also collapse the dollar. So he decided against it. It was a patriotic decision for which he got little credit at the time. But Churchill was concerned with the principle. "I cannot justify to my conscience the surrender now of part of our freedom," he stated on February 27th, "in the hope that it may be regained at some uncertain time in the future."

Describing the party decision as capitulation, he announced that he would sit as an independent Conservative. Actually he did not move from among his fellow Conservatives. But he did not run again in 1968.

The two Toronto Liberals who left the Trudeau party did it in stages. First, Perry Ryan expressed his disapproval of policies on defence and racial matters by sitting as an independent in 1969. But by September, 1970, he had decided he could support Robert Stanfield. He then moved across the floor to join the official opposition.

Paul Hellyer really moved in four stages. He resigned from the cabinet in 1969, mainly because his strong views on the need for better housing were ignored. In 1971 he took the second step and became an independent Liberal. Then he formed the political group, Action Canada, to promote better economic stability. Finally, in July 1972 he joined the Conservatives. He was re-elected in his own riding of Toronto-Trinity with just 183 votes to spare. Perry Ryan was defeated.

Roch Lasalle ran as a Conservative in Joliette, Quebec in 1965 and was defeated. He ran again in 1968 and made it, by just 172 votes. He sat with the Conservatives for three years. When Fernand Alie, president of the Quebec Conservative party proposed certain reforms in the party in 1971, Lasalle supported him. One of the proposals was revival of the principle of "deux nations," on which the party had nearly foundered in 1967 and 1968. Robert Stanfield had no inclination to renew a hopeless argument in semantics. He rejected major parts of Alie's proposals. Lasalle saw no alternative but to resign from the party and he did so on May 8th. He sat as an independent for the remainder of the parliament.

Roch Lasalle ran for re-election as an independent. He should never have done it. Independents just never get elected. Canadians do not approve of rebels and seldom send them back to parliament. Trudeau was riding high in Quebec and there was an offical Liberal candidate in Joliette. Lasalle only had a shaky majority of 172 to start with. But he ran anyway, and confounded everything I am trying to prove. He wiped out his nearest opponent, Liberal Claude Livernoche, by 5,255 votes.

Is there a new era coming for rebels? There is not much sign of it in Canada yet. But in Britain, the Common Market debate has forced new attitudes and a second look. If all the rebels had left or been forced out of their party, as they had in the past, the party system might have foundered. So the leaders had to grin and bear it. But few were happy about it.

"Any political party can sustain a few gymnasts," said Member William Price during the crisis, "but a whole circusful of them would be a disaster."

Most rebels in Canada change parties in stages. But not Raymond Rock. In March 1972, after 10 years as a Liberal Member, he crossed the floor directly to join the Conservatives. His main complaints were the lack of opportunity for private Members to present their views and the downgrading of constituency Members by the Prime Minister. He took a stand and risked his safe seat on the principle of representative government in Canada. The subsequent election proved that he was in tune with general Canadian opinion. There was a feeling that Trudeau had condensed his power into smaller groups and ignored his Members.

At the time he stood to announce his decision to leave the Liberals there was not much appreciation of his effort from their side. Following a lot of raucous comment in the House, Jack Cullen made the final remark from the government side.

"Lots of luck, fellows," he called over to the hooting Conservatives as the rebel made his way across the floor. Rock was a nuisance, and that is no prize possession in any party.

The sad thing is that his constituents seemed to feel the same way. Rather than rushing to support a courageous Member, they turned out in droves on election day 1972 to defeat him, two to one.

A little rebellion is a good thing in politics, as long as someone else does it.

THE HOSTS

"Almost Everyone Welcome"

Wednesday, May 18th, 1966, began like any other day on parliament hill. The fresh smell of spring was now in the air, dulled only faintly by fumes from across the river. The front lawn was green with new grass and the tulips were blooming around its borders. The massive front doors swung open at 9:00 a.m., signalling that the building was ready for visitors.

There is something different about stepping through that arched doorway into the Centre Block. The carved stone and marble foyer and hallways are like nothing else on earth. Here the visitor becomes a guest of the Members of Parliament. In this edifice the government is not in charge, and the Prime Minister, though treated with deference, is just another Member. The Speaker is offical host, and he has appointed about 90 staff members to greet visitors and show them around. And this staff is superb.

Today the 60 students from Pine Glen School, Huntsville, had their own Member waiting at the door. Principal Harold Taylor had made his plans well in advance. A visit to the mint and the war museum, and a tour of the experimental farm would be highlighted by sitting in on a session of the House of Commons. As the group arrived at 1:00 p.m. nobody there realized how exciting that session would turn out to be.

With the aid of an obliging protective staff member, the group was escorted to a committee room for an information session with their Member. Then the wide-eyed grade eighters went on a tour of the building, lined up in the corridor for the Speaker's parade at 2:00 p.m., and were finally settled in the south gallery to watch proceedings.

Shortly after two, the gallery door opened to admit another visitor. His name was Paul Chartier. He found an empty aisle seat beside the Pine Glen group and sat down barely noticed. After a while he got up and left. Chartier was also a guest of the Members, but an unwelcome one. For he had mass murder on his mind, and was carrying the means to accomplish it. Chartier didn't know much about explosives, but he had jammed about six inches of dynamite into a copper pipe and attached a fuse. He intended to throw it onto the floor of the House. When he left the gallery, he went to the adjacent washroom and lit the fuse. Then he started back to his seat in the gallery. But as he reached the washroom door, the home-made bomb, hidden under his jacket, went off. The washroom was demolished, and so was Chartier. He died almost instantly, about 2:50 p.m.

The sound of the blast could be heard in the Chamber and the windows shook. For a moment, Members thought that workmen were excavating somewhere on the hill. But almost immediately smoke appeared and the sharp smell of explosives drifted through the building. The students were so close to the detonation they felt the pressure of the blast. But only Chartier himself suffered injury.

When the Pine Glen students went home next day, they took as souvenirs pieces of splintered wood and shattered glass from the demolished washroom. And they also took something else. For in Chartier's room was found the piece of paper on which he had calculated the fuse time. A simple mistake in arithmetic had resulted in too short a fuse.

"That's a good lesson," principal Taylor said to his group. "Bad arithmetic cost that man his life."

"Yes, but I guess it was lucky for everyone else," said one of the students, and the principal could only agree.

People who want to be noticed have been throwing leaflets from the galleries for decades. But the paper is gathered up quickly and the culprit rushed out. So in August 1964 David Cowlishan tried something messy which couldn't be scooped up. As George Nowlan was speaking in the flag debate, Cowlishan threw a milk carton filled with animal blood onto the green carpeted centre aisle. Nowlan paused for just a moment in his remarks.

"It's all right, I don't think it's his heart's blood," he reassured the House. "I think it's his brains." Jack Bigg, however, voiced the thought on everyone's mind.

"It will be a live bomb next," he said, and he was nearly right.

Cowlishan paid for his untidiness. While leaflet throwers are warned and released, he was taken to court and fined.

One group of protesters made sure they wouldn't be thrown right out. On May 11th, 1970, 36 women from the Cross Canada Abortion Caravan suddenly chained themselves to seats throughout the galleries and snapped padlocks on the chairs. Then they started shouting at the Members, particularly Justice Minister John Turner, responsible for the abortion laws. One woman even managed to connect a microphone to the sound system, creating havoc with House business.

"Free abortion on demand," they cried out. "We want control of our bodies."

"Don't tell us, tell your parents," Bob McCleave called back, echoing the demand for retroactive abortion sometimes heard in the Chamber.

While the guards went out for wire cutters, the House adjourned for half an hour. The operation was so well-planned that many Members suspect inside advice. Gallery passes had been forged, the sound system penetrated and chains smuggled in. But nothing of this kind was proven. However, bolt cutters have been added to protective staff equipment. And they have come in handy, too. Just eleven months later, Mrs. Clare Culhane smuggled a chain and padlock into the gallery by zipping them into her high boots. Locking her ankle to a seat she threw leaflets and tried to ask questions of External Affairs Minister Mitchell Sharp. But it didn't last long. The bolt cutters quickly appeared and she was out in thirty seconds.

One way to prevent incidents is to keep people out. Yet parliament must be freely open to the public. Only once in recent years have the doors been closed. This was in May 1967 when a demonstration by nearly 10,000 farmers seemed to be getting out of hand. Representative groups were admitted to the buildings, but a lot more milled around outside, wanting in. As they became angry, and rushed towards the main doors, sergeant-at-arms David Currie ordered them closed. But it was drastic action in a drastic situation, and is very seldom required. Any kind of exclusion from the buildings results in protests. Roger Jay of the Union of Ontario Indians arrived at the main door in March 1972 with a bundle of press releases.

It seemed to him innocent enough. He was going to deliver them to a press gallery reporter for distribution. But he was taken into custody, and had to wait until the reporter came for him. The fact that he was an Indian representing Indians, and exposing the lack of health services in Northern Ontario was embarrassing. And the Speaker expressed regrets over the incident. But Jay had run up against two problems. The first was a security matter. Bringing a parcel into the buildings is not permitted. The second was a prohibition against door-to-door distribution of literature. That was not his intention, but the staff could not know. Long memories recalled enforcement of the ban ten years earlier, when messengers from the Bank of Canada tried to distribute James Coyne's controversial statements. How was Jay to know all this? He couldn't.

"I guess they thought I was in the Mafia," he said, passing off the incident. But he was hurt, as are all those who break the rules.

Others who are hurt by safety precautions are the Members themselves. When foreign heads of state arrive, tight security is enforced. The RCMP patrols the approaches to the buildings. While the Commons staff know the Members by sight, the Mounties do not. So there is always a howl when a Member is stopped on his way into parliament. He is entitled to free entry without question. Furthermore, detention of politicians on the pretext of identity is a practice in some controlled states. It can not be allowed here. It would be relatively simple for a Commons guard to stand at the appropriate entrance with the Mountie. But this always seems to be overlooked by security forces, to whom everyone is suspect. Some of the most outraged speeches result from holding up Members who want to get to their offices. But they must protest. So must everyone else improperly barred. So where does that leave the security forces, who are only trying to protect everyone? Just ask them; they have an expression for it.

Sometimes the problem is reversed. "Who pushed Stephen Juba?" was the mystery around the hill in February 1969. The Mayor of Winnipeg had no trouble getting into the buildings. His problem was getting out. After leaving the office of James Richardson he apparently got lost. He asked a guard for directions and was told he should not be in that part of the building. What part? Juba doesn't know, and the guard was never identified. But some words were exchanged and Juba later complained that the guard pushed him. The Mayor pushed back and the guard went off for help. Juba then found his way out fast enough.

"If I had stayed, they might have taken me off in handcuffs," he later explained.

Patrick Sayers thought he would wake people up around parliament, but it got him into trouble. An Ojibway from Sault Ste. Marie, he burned with frustration over injustices. Things that had happened to him. Things that had happened to others. So he went to Ottawa to do something about it. But his angry attitude and language got him nowhere. On April 8th, 1970, he fixed up a little fire bomb and dropped it in the east stairwell. It made some smoke and caused the desired excitement.

The fire bomb caused people to think, all right, but along the wrong lines for Patrick. He was charged with creating a public nuisance and pleaded guilty in court a month later. As he waited for his case, he imagined himself outlining his grand catalogue of complaints. But it didn't happen that way. His lawyer spoke for him, but without the personal sense of wrong Patrick felt. The judge seemed more interested in what happened on April 8th than in the entire history of wrongs suffered by the Indian people. Feeling that the public had to be protected from these dangerous acts, Judge René Marin sentenced Sayers to nine months in jail.

"I didn't have a chance to give my side of it," Sayers protested, remembering all the things he had come to say.

"I've already passed sentence on this matter," ruled the judge, "and I don't intend to debate it further."

"You're making a mockery of justice, you fascist puppet," shouted Sayers, revealing a great deal in his use of language.

Judge Marin contained himself, and told Sayers he could decide whether he wanted to apologize. He was taken from the court room to meditate. But all he could think of was injustice.

"This court perpetuates injustices," said Sayers when he was brought back. "I don't wish to apologize." So the judge added three months for contempt of court, and Sayers was led away, unvindicated.

Violence seldom makes the wheels turn faster, even in parliament.

Custom requires visitors to the House galleries to be "modestly" dressed. But rapid changes in fashions and morals make it tough for the protective staff. For years, shorts were prohibited in the galleries. But as they became accepted female summer attire, visitors in shorts were admitted and allowed to sit in the back rows. As the seventies arrived, so did "hot pants." Visibly little different from the bottom half of a bathing suit, modesty was achieved by an accompanying skirt or jacket, split to the navel. The protective staff had this one figured. It was immodest. Then someone raised the question of where shorts ended and hot pants began. With visions of having to take measurements, the guards backed down.

"If they have it covered, they can bring it in," was the tentative decision.

Maryann Gray didn't exactly know the rules, but she knew her hot pants were pretty hot. So when she arrived for Englehart with her high school group in May 1971, she wore a white leather jacket over her tight pants and red cashmere sweater. But you can't wear a coat into the galleries. It's too easy to conceal a weapon under it. So when Maryann got to the gallery door, she was asked to take off her coat and check it. She complied and walked in. Another guard spotted her almost immediately.

"You can't come into the gallery like that," he said, "go out and cover up."

So she went out, and got her white coat again. Since it was now quite obvious that nothing was concealed under it, they let her wear it. This is just one of the great efforts made in the House of Commons to protect its Members from danger.

Some visitors don't come to watch proceedings, tour the buildings, protest or throw things. They come to kill themselves, with as much publicity as possible. While some members are verbally doing the same thing in the Chamber, these people choose the Peace Tower. A jump from the public observation gallery just under the clock face results in certain death. Until the mid-sixties, nothing prevented a person from climbing the five foot wall and jumping over. Then metal bars were installed to prevent that. But these only provided a challenge for Ronald Heatley. Depressed by personal problems and possibly influenced by hashish, he managed to squeeze through the bars and jump to his death on April 1st, 1970.

"He didn't think he would hit the ground," said a friend Joyce Dunn, who was with him.

The coroner at the inquest wanted to learn why Heatley died. But the jury made no finding. So it will never be known whether he jumped under the influence of drugs or sought publicity for his own self-destruction.

If there was any doubt about Heatley, there was none about the next one who tried. For sheer persistence, she was unsurpassed. Himani Ghosh came from India in 1967 to be married. But the plans were cancelled. For two years she was unemployed, and though she finally got work, she was still depressed. She was not happy in Canada, but would not return to India. Finally she decided to commit suicide in Canada's most central and conspicuous place. Perhaps Heatley's successful effort three months earlier had something to do with it. In any case, she went up to the tower and got her head through the bars, but could get no farther. Then a guard came along.

"It's a beautiful view," she said, then left.

Five days later, on July 22nd, she was back. This time she tried it feet first, but got stuck again. A guard saw her this time as well, but she had a story.

"I just want to go out on the corner tower to pray," she explained.

She came back two days later and asked for a chair, to get a better view. It was refused. Though different guards were on tower duty each time, she was now suspect. As she moved from exit to exit, the guard kept his eye on her. There was no excuse to evict her, but she had to be watched. When the tower guards changed, she was still there. Now she was interfering with staff duties. She had declined to leave and the staff was reluctant to use force. They could see the headlines: "Foreign visitor attacked by parliament's protective staff." So after four hours, they announced the tower was being closed. There was no further excuse to stay, so she left. As soon as she had departed, it was opened again.

Three days later, she was back. This time she was lucky, for her own purposes at least. The guard had just come back from holidays, and didn't know her. As Harold Carter was talking to some other visitors, she got a chair, and made her final try. This time, she knew what to do. She somehow squeezed through an opening 7 inches wide by 13 inches high, and was free of the world's trials.

Nobody else has maaged the trick since then, because more bars have been added. Now visitors see the Gatineau Hills, the Ottawa River, and the national capital through bars like a prison door. It's a pity really.

There has to be a limit to protection. That limit was passed during the FLQ incident. There were those who felt that the government over-reacted, and I was one. Some risks have to be taken, and some principles must be maintained in time of crisis. So when the army moved inside the buildings on October 12th, 1970 to protect the Members, I protested. Crises, either real or manufactured, have always been the excuse for curtailment of movement. In this case, fortunately, Defence Minister Donald Macdonald agreed, and the troops were withdrawn. These are unwelcome guests in any free assembly.

Finally, some guests create comment without saying or doing anything. Thus Charlotte Whitton arrived in the gallery one day, shortly after she became Conservative candidate to run against George McIlraith in Ottawa West. Her independence, biting tongue and unpredictable stands usually kept those associated with her in turmoil. On this occasion McIlraith happened to be making a partisan speech.

"Just wait till Charlotte gets you," jibed a Conservative Member to McIlraith.

"Just wait till you get Charlotte," replied a Liberal gleefully.

And that made it even.

The Members have a lot of guests. In 1967, centennial year, over a million people went through the main doors to have a look around. In other years it averages about 650,000. Some misbehave. But it is a very small percentage.

For most Members, the real joy and challenge as a host is in meeting groups of students. They can get pretty critical sometimes, and rightly so.

"There are plenty of things wrong around here," Members concede, "I hope you are stirred up enough to run some day yourself. This is the place where the changes must be made."

Every election brings in new Members determined to succeed.

149

THE PAYOFF

"Votes, That Is"

Grafters, crooks and influence-peddlers. That's what all the old stories and jokes infer about politicians. The possibility of being labelled that way keeps a lot of people out of active politics.

"It must be tough when political friends split," says one.

"Not when they split 50-50," is the reply.

And the rich uncle story.

"I worked hard for 40 years and never got ahead," says the uncle.

"Where did you get all your money, then?"asks the nephew.

"Oh, I spent a couple of years in politics."

And finally, the one that is used to fit any occasion.

"She knows my father's in jail, my mother's a drunk and my sister's on the street," says the bridegroom. "But I just can't tell her about my brother in politics."

Well, these are told in good fun, and everybody laughs: but some people still wonder how much truth there is in them.

It was from Tammany Hall that the picture developed and the stories circulated throughout North America. For 70 years, until Fiorella LaGuardia became mayor in 1934, New York city was run on the "ward boss" system by that club of leading Democrats. There was no hypocrisy in the idea. The machine was designed to win elections and divide the spoils. You went to the district leader for a job, a pushcart license, a bucket of coal when things were tough, help in filling out forms and bailing relatives out of jail. In return, he wanted your vote and loyal support. For bigger favours or commercial deals, suitable returns to the election fund and a cash payment to the negotiator were expected. The idea was not repugnant to many European immigrants, accustomed to powerful local rulers at home. National issues, social reform or

150

ideology played no part — just the ability to stay on the winning side. This was raw politics at the basic level. It is disappearing throughout North America at various rates of speed. But the public is confused as to just what stage it has reached in any particular region.

To sell influence, you first must have it.

A couple of weeks after I was elected in 1957, I went to Ottawa to find out what influence I really had. "On small construction jobs under $5,000, name your man," said the Public Works officer. "We will give him the job on a time and material basis. On larger ones, we have to put out tenders."

"We will accept your recommendation for small office appointments," said the post office man. "The larger offices are civil service competitions."

So it went. Throughout the public service of Canada, the small jobs and minor appointments in the riding were the prerogative of a government supporter. Though not much, it was something for Members on the winning side. But that was before Howard Green and Bill Hamilton got a grip on their departments of Public Works and Post Office. Sick to death of Liberal patronage while they were in opposition, each vowed to end it. Everything would be done by public tender, competitive examination or civil service appointement.

And it was. Within about two years, over the loud wails of expectant supporters, and harried Members, the small vestige of the spoils system disappeared in Canada.

Now, a recommendation from the Member is likely to do more harm than good. The public service pretends to believe that an applicant goes to his Member when he can't get the job on merit.

So everything is now on the up-and-up in public appointments? Not exactly. They have been removed from the Members, who at least had to answer for their actions. Now they are shuffled around within the bureaucracy, which has its own patronage system, and nobody to finger for blunders.

But the old idea dies hard, and the pressure for patronage jobs is constant. "I have worked for your election in four campaigns, believing you a fair man," a constituent wrote. "I never asked for anything in return. But now I would like this little job as part-time caretaker. Nobody else around here wants it."

Knowing the man to be reliable, I wrote a letter of recommendation. Suddenly discovering the position open, the public service commission set up a "competition." They managed to find someone else.

"I can't understand it," wrote my man again. "You gave the job to someone who has a long way to travel, and is no good anyway. Either you don't know him, or you don't trust me."

What kind of an examination can you dream up for a part-time caretaker? It was really reliability that counted. Explanations to the constituent were hopeless. He believed his Member had some influence. The appointee turned out useless, and had to be replaced.

It's easy to see why no private Member has recently been accused of influence peddling.

Constant pressure, however can result in obtaining public works. There is still a vague idea around that this gets votes. Build a dock here, a post office there, and everybody in the area will vote for you. Help someone get a position and all his relatives will love you. Expectant recipients like to encourage the idea, but experienced Members know better. It's best illustrated by a favourite story in political circles.

The Member meets one of his supporters, and finds him grumpy. "What are you going to do for me?" asks the constituent. "I'm not sure I'll vote for you this time."

"But I got that new post office built in your village," says the Member, "and we bought the land from your brother."

"I know, but that did nothing for me."

"You've been trucking on government jobs for five years," replies the Member. "Didn't I get you on through the foreman?"

"That's true," replied the constituent, "but what have you done for me recently?"

With so much government beneficence floating around these days, the value is dropping for the Member. He gets much less personal credit.

"It's about time they did something," is the usual reward for months of effort.

But the exceptions prove the rule. I was discussing these ideas with publisher Jack McClelland early in 1972. "You know I just cannot understand Jim Richardson making such a fuss about getting the Mint in Winnipeg," he commented. "Here's a man who is well off, urbane, sensible and a cabinet minister. It's funny what politics will do to a person."

He was right. And Richardson must have felt the same way. But following the October election, Richardson was one of the few Liberal Members in the west who survived. And getting the Mint for Winnipeg was a big factor in his survival. He is still at it.

One way or another, a Member has to prove that he has some authority.

And in the general area of getting things for his riding, most are successful. But the desired result is not in favours from friends, nor a payoff in money. It is getting a good share of government spending and public attention for his area. The payoff is in votes. And that is really all a Member wants.

There is less need now for underhanded financial returns. Reasonable salary scales, and retirement pensions remove the necessity of grabbing extra dollars. There was a time when low salaries seemed to invite a Member to sell his influence. Several recent increases have remedied that, but raised public expectations in other areas.

Two letters reached my office a few days after the 1971 salary increase.

"Now that you are getting more money, you can spend more time in Ottawa," said one.

"Maybe we'll see more of you around the riding," commented the other.

They couldn't both win.

No matter how hard Members try to resist favouritism, people pressure them towards it.

"Here's another of those letters praising Mr. Jones," said secretary Billie Grey, going through the mail. "It's from the same place and worded the same way. I guess this relative forgot to mail hers right away."

Letter-writing campaigns are pressure by volume. Prime Ministers, party leaders and Members are greatly influenced by the mail they get. But they tend to look for the motivation. A petition with 50 names may come from one person who is concerned and 49 others who would rather sign than argue. Signatures or names on a bundle of pre-printed cards may represent fulfillment of a duty to the union. Even a number of hand-written letters may be the brainchild of one person if sent from the same place, at the same time, and worded the same way. A few individually written letters, from people the Member can identify, carry a lot more weight. They aren't pressure, they are genuine opinion.

The volume and verdict of letters can be deceiving. When Raymond Rock left the Liberal Party in 1972 on a matter of principle, his correspondents agreed with his action.

"About 54 per cent of my constituents support me," he concluded in May 1972 after receiving a large amount of mail. But when election day came, only 30 per cent said it in votes.

A lot of individual letters seek to apply pressure on the Member through anger. Some people think that hostile letters and threats will scare him into special consideration.

"I have often read with disgust about your putrid actions in Ottawa," wrote Mr. Culp, then went on to ask a favour.

"After being so dirty, and doing me out of what's coming to me," wrote Mr. Brooks, "don't expect any votes around here. However, you could try again."

"I got your letter of congratulations, which was very small," wrote Mrs. Elliott. "I thought you would send me a silver dollar or something I could show people. I also had a nice letter from the Queen; she could have sent a brooch or necklace which she would never miss."

"Dear Sir or Madam, as the case may be," began the sarcastic handwritten note, inferring lack of guts.

A Member has one great advantage. Nobody can fire him. He is subject to no job control, no superior attitudes. He cannot be called on the carpet, and told, "Sorry, buddy, but what you have been saying is out of line; change your tune or find a new job." When the pressures get heavy, it's a great feeling. "You can push me, watch me, get mad at me, and write dirty letters; but you can't fire me," he thinks some tired afternoon at six o'clock.

"Go to hell!"

A few Members do get into trouble over alleged personal gain, but they are mostly ministers. Failure by minister René Tremblay to pay promptly for furniture purchased in the scandal-ridden mid-sixties raised an inference that it was an improper gift. Yvon Dupuis was asked to resign in 1965 over race-track money, though he denied any wrong-doing.

The real problems arise because almost everybody now deals with government.

A cabinet minister is bound to have some friends, relatives or associates dealing routinely with his department. Thus it was recently shown that a government contract was awarded Edgar Benson's old accounting firm when he was still in the cabinet. Margaret Haidasz, daughter of minister Stanley Haidasz, applied for an Opportunities for Youth grant. Ministers seldom have any knowledge of individual applications for government assistance. They are concerned with policy. This is illustrated by the unhappy case in Ontario of D'Arcy McKeough. As minister responsible for land planning, his name was stamped daily on dozens of plans which had gone through departmental routine. He neither saw them nor knew about them. One day some family members applied, as they must, for approval of a plan. In due course, his name was stamped on it. In August 1972, a newspaper became critical. A man of absolute integrity, McKeough resigned; a great loss to the public. Fortunately for Ontario, he was soon reinstated.

It is even impossible for a private Member, who makes no executive decisions, to avoid some conflict of interest.

If you are drawing old age security and vote for an increase, is that conflict of interest?

If you are a farmer, and vote for price supports, don't you benefit personally?

If you hold shares in a public company and vote them a benefit, what is that? Nothing, as long as you don't hold too many shares.

Everything seems to depend on the time and circumstances. Sometimes there is no reaction at all to allegations of conflict. At other times a mere whisper escalates to trouble. Eddie Asselin was a popular Member from Montreal. He had a gallant air force record, a successful business background and long public service. One day in 1965 it was disclosed that prior to his election, he had made a fast profit in a real estate deal — nothing very unusual in the sixties. But since he had been on city council, and school property was involved, fingers were pointed. There was some inference that he had done something wrong, and might do it again. So as to cause no embarrassment to scandal-laden Lester

Pearson, he dropped out. So far as I can recall, he was the only private Member to do so.

How do Canadians view the activities of their Members? Very well, in general. Not long ago, Paddy Robertson, actress and columnist, asked me what a Member's priorities are supposed to be.

"It's never been laid out, exactly," I answered.

"Well, why don't you find out what the people think?" she countered. "Then you will know how you are doing."

So I sent out a questionnaire to 500 Canadians. Their names were taken at random from telephone books in every province and the territories. One hundred and sixteen replied. In one place, criticism was invited. Though some considered Members overpaid and self-seeking, not one person suggested dishonesty or graft in their comments. That speaks well for both Members and the public.

There is a constant struggle for influence between Member and government. Ministers and their departments would like to keep everything out of the Members' grasp. This takes away temptation for payoff, they pretend. But it gives the power to people who have no personal contact with the public, and who can hide their mistakes in anonymity. Members must account.

The Opportunities for Youth program put the Member's influence exactly where the government wants it. The Program originated as the seventies began, to give disillusioned young Canadians a sense of participation. Hastily set up as a new section of the bureaucracy, with novices approving expenditure of millions of dollars on "youth" projects, it immediately ran foul of almost everybody.

The professional civil servants were appalled at the methods used. The Members were shocked at the type of projects approved. Local governments were annoyed when their plans were by-passed for off-beat experiments by immature youth. The public was upset by odd-ball social programs financed with their tax money.

Worst of all, however, hords of young Canadians became more disillusioned than ever. These were the ones whose applications were refused. The "come one, come all" invitation was accepted by all. There was only money for a fraction of them. With fuzzy guidelines the instant bureaucrats went for off-beat projects which appealed to them. The others were not even acknowledged.

One thing the originators of OFY did not want, was to have Members involved. Regarded as prototypes of the generation gap, they would foul up the whole thing for sure. The first year found Members bewildered as federal projectlets popped up around them like mushrooms.

With universal criticism and an approaching election, the government had to share the blame for the 1972 program with somebody. So they shoved it neatly onto the Members. Sending each one a long list of applications from his riding, with no details whatever, the ministry invited comment. They paid no attention whatever to the replies they got. Some Members avoided the trap. Others who diligently looked into projects, and objected to some, found those very ones approved. The ones they liked were rejected. But the government had an out. They had "consulted." They tried it again in 1973, but this time they refined the system a bit. Letters of rejection explained that the Member had been consulted. The reaction from the Members was violent.

"All we attempted was to explain the process," pleaded Secretary of State Hugh Faulkner when the storm broke in May.

"It's reprehensible," charged Erik Nielsen.

"Straight dishonesty," added George Hees.

"Consultation does not mean that the Member has the final say," added the Minister. "I do."

The influence vehicle was running a rough course. But with its hand firmly on the wheel, the government could blame the bumps on the back-seat drivers.

THE PRESS

"Give Us a Line, Fellows"

On his way to the television studio one winter day in Ottawa, Paul St. Pierre was reviewing his knowledge of the Organization of American States. As parliamentary secretary to the Minister, he was expected to have his facts straight. No guesswork, no offhand comments. Canada's position towards the OAS has always been ambiguous. A false assumption, a careless word on his part could make it worse; even cause international complications. As he was guest on a CBC program, the coverage would be national. No doubt the interviewer would do his best to trip him up. But as he arrived, Paul felt confident that he could handle any questions.

When the cameras rolled, Paul was completely thrown off. What did he think about Trudeau calling B.C. Premier Bennett a bigot, the interviewer wanted to know. What's this? Of course Paul had some ideas but how to express them? As he wound a hazardous course through the maze of questions, the time was suddenly gone. The Organization of American States wasn't discussed.

"They'll have a hard time getting me on a show again," he said disgustedly as he left for the parliament buildings.

Robert Thompson was campaigning for the Progressive Conservatives in his home province of Alberta. A candidate in British Columbia, he could feel a surge of support for the party rising in the west. Trudeau would never be able to form a majority government, and could easily lose. Thompson held a news conference to express his optimism.

"What would happen to the leadership if the Conservatives are decisively beaten?" asked a reporter.

"We're not going to lose," he replied confidently.

"But the issue has been raised in Prince Albert," insisted his questioner. "Bill Fair says there is a fight going on for party leadership."

"A decisive defeat would definitely mean a leadership convention, no question about that," Thompson acknowledged, drawing on his store of political experience. "But we are not going to lose."

It was a hypothetical question, answered honestly and confidently. His intent was clear. But here was the two line caption in Toronto's Globe and Mail:

MOVE TO OUST STANFIELD SEEN
IF TORIES ARE BEATEN DECISIVELY

The first line, read by itself, is devastating during an election campaign. And going on to the second line, the possibility of a decisive defeat is "revealed."Thompson never intended to put it that way. But the editor undoubtedly did.

Robert Stanfield was making a pre-election visit to Parry Sound-Muskoka. The timetable took him to Parry Sound on July 8th, the time and place of the annual Orange parade. As the light aircraft carrying Stanfield, candidate Stan Darling, and a couple of press men approached Parry Sound, it began a long delaying circuit.

"What's the hold-up?" asked a reporter, raising his voice against the engine noise.

"We don't want to arrive until the parade is over," I called out, from the seat beside the pilot. There was no point in trying to compete with the parade which was just ending near our destination at the dock. And arrival shortly after the parade ended has several advantages. Timing was perfect, and everything went well. Until next morning.

"A tour organizer, MP Gordon Aiken, said they wanted no meeting with the Orangemen," Canadian Press man Gray wrote of the delay. This started off a flood of controversy. He wasn't exactly wrong, but the way he put it attracted attention. A Globe and Mail editorial writer had a brain wave for a heading "Bananaman meets Orangemen" and had to write something under it. Leslie Saunders, Toronto's defender of the ancient order, had to write a letter to the editor; and others had to reply. My older relatives of Northern Ireland ancestry felt badly let down. It took weeks for the dust to settle. And the sad part was that Stan Darling, for whom the tour was organized, didn't even get mentioned.

Jack Marshall saw a flaw in the proposed Family Income Security Plan. There are cases where children are not in custody of their mother. In such cases, Marshall reasoned, payments should be made to the guardian. So he moved an amendment allowing payments to be made to a trustee for the children. "Marshall wants money to be paid direct to children," his proposal was reported.

Nobody who read the amendment or heard his explanation could have taken that from it.

"I was never approached about it," said Jack. "Maybe they didn't want to spoil a story by finding out the facts."

These are four examples from 1972 of the game of questions and answers. Pulling a switch; the hypothetical question; the equivocal phrase, and the unconfirmed report are favourite games. There are plenty more. Members don't like this kind of reporting. It makes them look foolish for one thing, and leaves a poor impression with the public. Also it costs a lot in time, answering the unconstructive criticism which results. It is true that some Members believe in the theory that, "It doesn't matter what they say, as long as they're talking about me."

Their specialty is controversy and they can find lots of it. But even they like to pick their own subjects, and fight on their own grounds.

"The most exclusive club in the country" is a phrase sometimes used to describe the Members in their confines on parliament hill. But the parliamentary press gallery is ahead on almost all scores. Numbering less than 150, they report on everything and everybody in parliament, except themselves. Representatives of large dailies and news chains, T.V. and radio reporters, opinionated columnists, straight news gatherers and foreign correspondents, they have a frightening power potential. Diverse in their opinions, attitudes and allegiance, they normally cancel each other out. But now and then, driven by some unexplained force, they all move off in a common direction. The pipeline debate of 1956, the elevation and destruction of John Diefenbaker, the scandals of the Pearson regime, the Trudeaumania of 1968 and his fall from grace in 1972 were pressed forward by gallery promotion.

The groundwork is done by the columnists and commentators. News selection is done by the others. It doesn't take long for the mood to spread to editors, local reporters and feature writers. The sustained attack on John Diefenbaker in 1961 and 1962 was terrifying to behold. Any reporter who wanted in on the act could find a place on "Preview Commentary" or any national program. But if he said a good word about the government, he didn't get a second chance. And the power stands unabated.

"Trudeaumania, after all, was largely an invention of the press," wrote Dennis Braithwaite in the Toronto Star in October 1972. "It has vanished not because the man has changed, but because the reporters don't want to play that game any more."

Braithwaite said also that reporters are human, and they like and respect the people who seem to like and respect them. Right. It's the same with the Members, both leaders and followers. Some press gallery members make a special effort for private Members.

Geoff Scott has been doing television interviews with Members for ten years. It's a personal kind of operation, getting opinions, views and comments on major and human interest events. Though his broadcast area is south-west Ontario, he interviews any Member. He records their own words and there is little room for misunderstanding.

Ron Collister has been around the gallery over 10 years. He reports fairly and accurately, and gives private Members credit for their efforts.

Art Blakeley is an old hand in the gallery. He writes good stuff, and has a national reputation. But he is still friendly and helpful. He is really interested in Members' views; not just those that support his own.

George Bain tends to be a little opinionated, but his opinions are valid. He is not jealous of the Members and often jumps to their defence.

Farmer Tissington takes a personal interest in "his" Members. If your riding is served by one of his papers, your speeches and comments will be reported. Sometimes he even sees more in a speech than the Member did.

Fraser MacDougall is an old hand in the gallery, does factual reporting and is well-liked.

That's why these six rated on top when I asked Members to grade the press gallery in 1972. And for the same reasons, others rated high. Vic Mackie, Stu MacLeod, Clement Brown, Peter Desbarats, John Drewry, Ken Mason, Maurice Western, Larry Zolf, Jean Marc Poliquin, David Crane and Peter Ward appeared in that order. Bub Hull, who had left the gallery to edit an Owen Sound daily, was included. These are all reporters who have been around a while, and maintain good relations with the Members. Though some run critical comments, they are considered fair. Further down the list were those who have less contact with the Members. At the bottom were those considered over-critical, dangerous to talk with or careless with facts. Members are human too. They can stand criticism if they deserve it. But they much prefer positive reports of what they are trying to accomplish. Reporters have to be pretty solid in the business to be objective and still get printed. The press gallery has men like that.

The absence of a few well-known names from the list of favourites shows how sensitive the Members are. Some reporters remain aloof and report critically. It's a necesssary part of a free press. Press gallery members have full status in the buildings. They sit in the coffee shop and palaver with the Members and among themselves. But Members' attitudes with the press are ambivalent. They would like to be reported, but not adversely. Press competition is keen and an unguarded remark could easily turn into a nasty headline. New men in the gallery, as well as new Members, want to make a name for themselves. They don't get it by fair comment. For the new boys, then, it's a bit of a stand-off. For the old timers, there's a more comfortable rapport among those who understand each other.

You have to say this for all the press gallery. They work hard. Like the Members, they are never off duty. They must have a wide knowledge of all aspects of political affairs. Without notice, they get huge volumes of royal commission reports, the public accounts, the budget, government policy statements and committee findings dropped in their laps. They must comment quickly and accurately, and a lot of the background must be in their heads. Editors sometimes ruin good reporting efforts. Space, news priorities and personal bias result in a good item being cut. Next day it's not news, so it disappears.

There is no doubt the news media play favourites among the Members. Some of the reasons are obvious. Those Members who are always coming up with new ideas, quotable expressions and a quaint turn of phrase are newsworthy. So are those who blurt things out while others are thinking about them. Odd-ball ideas and strong language get wide coverage. All this is to be expected, though it's a disappointment to those who take responsible positions and make serious, if dull, speeches.

Sometimes there is something deeper and much more sinister. Leaks from caucus and inside tip-offs to press men are often repaid by special mention in news stories. Generally it is a one-to-one deal, but sometimes it is bigger than that. The leaks may be planted to learn public reaction to a proposal under consideration.

It may be something else entirely. I learned this personally a few years ago when a parliamentary committee was looking into safety features and pollution control devices in automobiles. We had hearings in Windsor and were then invited informally to see the big manufacturing plants in Detroit. There was a CBC crew with us on the tour, and one company absolutely refused to let them through the gate. Competition being what it is, no secrets were getting out of that place by word or picture. The security staff converged on the crew and held them virtual prisoners.

The whole thing seemed ridiculous to me. Members were certainly not being shown any secrets. The news people were only doing their job, and wanted something to show for their trip other than people getting on and off buses. So I intervened on their behalf. When security remained stubborn, I got stubborn too. I refused to go on the tour until some working rules were outlined for the press. Some of my colleagues thought me a bit silly, and took off on the tour anyway. But the fuss was embarrassing enough that things were sorted out, and the CBC crew finally got permission to take some pictures inside.

For some time after that incident, I appeared to be one of parliament's most active Members. Every time the public turned on their T.V. or radio, there I was, commenting on the events of the day. It was a great new experience. I didn't have to say anything silly or shocking to hit the air waves. Good serious comment was presented as good serious comment. I glowed in my new-found popularity for several weeks, until that particular crew broke up and its members moved on to other fields. Then I went back to being just another Member, trying to catch attention without being too ridiculous.

"The unnamed questioner" is the bit that drives some Members to despair. Having special expertise in a particular subject, the opposition critic detects special activity in a department. So he frames a careful question and hits the jackpot.

"Yes," replies the Minister, "we have developed a new policy on that matter, and will shortly introduce legislation."

It's headline news. But the person who dug it out is not mentioned. "Answering a question in the House. . ." begins the article, and goes on to quote the Minister's words. While the reporter undoubtedly mentioned the Member's name, the editor really didn't think it important. And it's not just opposition Members either. A good Minister may drop a hint to a government supporter which results in a jackpot question. But only the reply is published. As far as the editor is concerned, the seal can just go on with his desk-pounding.

But why are all these people so news-hungry? Surely grown men and women are past the thrill of seeing their name in the paper. Well, the news media provide the best pipeline to the people. Unreported, the effort is wasted. Nobody knows what Members are doing, or whether they are doing anything. They ask questions, make speeches and present ideas, but generally it's talking to empty space. A hundred visitors in the gallery aren't going to influence public opinion. Neither are those few thousand who read Hansard two or three days later. But if your idea is picked from something like 25 questions and 15 speeches made each day, you have scored. It's tough when they don't even mention who shot the puck.

Let's go to the final beef, and then sum up. After pencilling out the names of questioners who aren't that important; after chopping articles about Members he hasn't heard of; after headlining the abusive exchanges and ignoring the serious speeches, what does the editor do?

"Where is Mr. Stanfield's team?" asked a Globe and Mail editorial writer in March 1972, professing to have heard of only five or six of his Members. "Under your blue pencil," the Members could reply, "and on the editorial floor."

Editors have asked the same question of other opposition leaders seeking to form a government. "Who have you got?" they ask. "We never heard of anybody but the leader and a couple of others."

And this is the opposition, who get to ask all the leading questions, make the critical speeches and get nasty with the government. What about Members on the government side who don't have those opportunities? Unless they make a wild statement, vote against the government, or leave the party, they are hardly worth mentioning. And that's not really the kind of publicity they want.

So what does the public think of their boobs of Members, misquoted, unquoted, silly or never heard of? I mentioned earlier a little survey we did. Included was the question: "Are MP's properly reported?" Here are the answers to that one.

Yes	20
No	27
Often Misrepresented	48
Total replies	95

It is obvious that the people are ready to make some allowances for bad reporting. And that is something for which Members can be thankful!

Though they would probably recoil in horror at the thought, Canada's press men give an effective assist in keeping the Members in line. Dissent within the ranks is treated as startling, unusual and worthy of a blow-by-blow description. The perpetrator is viewed with wonder and amazement. In a few cases, he gets the hero's role, but more often he is the villain. Unless he thrives on turbulence and controversy, he is much better to keep quiet. "Step out of line," says the press man, "and you are available to get clobbered. You may manage to dodge, hide or get away clean if you are lucky. But you have become news and that's our business. If we stretch things a bit, don't be surprised."

Members know that in saying anything at all, they take their chances. But they must be reported, seen and heard. So they keep right on talking, knowing the press will find plenty of chaff among the wheat.

THE CRUSADERS

"Keep Trying"

Whenever Reynold Rapp stood up to make a speech in Parliament, someone would call out: "Rapp is for rape."

Showing no signs of annoyance at the obvious insult, Reynold would smile benignly and go on with his remarks. He knew, and so did his heckler, that it merely drew attention to his crusade. During the war, rapeseed oil had a flourishing market as a lubricant. It became a cash crop in Northern Saskatchewan and the Peace River district of Alberta. But following war's end, the demand faltered. New hope for growers soon developed with an increased demand for vegetable oils. Rapeseed is rich in oil and could compete for the new markets. But there was one serious drawback. It was not recognized as a grain under the Railway Act, and did not qualify for the special Crows nest Pass haulage rates. Thus it was in danger of losing out to more profitable western crops, as well as to competitors in other countries. In the midst of these new developments, Reynold Rapp had been elected in 1958 as the Member for Saskatchewan riding of Humboldt-Melfort, a rapeseed area. Offhand, he didn't fit the bill for the obvious task. Small of stature, and unassuming, he spoke hesitantly with an accent recalling his birth and education in the Crimea. But he revealed his innermost thoughts during his first speech given three weeks after his arrival in Ottawa. It was heart-warming in its emotion and simplicity, and revealed a deep commitment.

"When I arrived here in Ottawa for the first time and walked across from Union Station to Parliament Hill I was all eyes," he said. "My heart was filled with emotion when I saw the graceful parliament buildings, the statues and the other historic sights. The first statue that I walked up to was that of Sir Wilfrid Laurier, the great French-Canadian statesman and as I looked up I could almost see a twinkle in his eyes. I thought I could hear him say these words:

166

What are you, a little immigrant of just 29 years' residence, here in Ottawa for? Didn't I hear you say that all you wanted from life was to come to Canada and make a home for youself and your family? I thought you were very content when Canada had given you this opportunity and your life's ambition was achieved. But now I see you are here as the new Member for Humboldt-Melfort to represent this great constituency in the 24th parliament. As this is the case, go on then, and do the job assigned to you for the glory of Canada and your constituency.

Then he reached the statue of Sir John A. Macdonald and thought of Canada as a country where he had the right to work, prosper and shape his own destiny without interference or state control.

"I make a solemn pledge to safeguard these virtues and to preseve these high principles," he told the House, "until the time arrives to pass them on to those who follow us."

Not satisfied to be an ordinary citizen, Reynold Rapp was not satisfied to be an ordinary Member, either. He soon began his crusade for rapeseed. He talked about it in the House, in caucus, to the press. With Ged Baldwin, Member for Peace River, he took the case to the Board of Transport Commissioners. But by a split decision, the Board decided that rapeseed did not qualify for the special rates under the law as it stood. So he proposed a bill to change the law. His bill was not reached. He lobbied with the ministry. Nothing seemed to be getting through. But he did have a friend of western agriculture in court — fellow Saskatchewan Member John Diefenbaker, who also happened to be Prime Minister. Even he had his problems. The railways had to be persuaded to take a reduction in revenues. But finally on June 20th, 1961 Leon Balcer, Minister of Transport, rose in the House to present bill C111.

"The purpose of this bill," he announced, "is to apply to rapeseed the railway freight rates applicable under the Crowsnest Pass agreement."

That was it. The government bill went through quickly and the crusade was well launched. Rapeseed is now a $200 million annual crop, of which half is exported. Reynold Rapp was not the only person pushing the issue, but he was the most visible — and the most persistent. By all standards, he was also the most fortunate. He had realized his objective in three years.

Almost every Member has his own personal crusade. It is something special to him. It goes beyond the routine of parliamentary business and riding representation. In many cases, it is the issue that brought him into politics. And if he is persistent enough, people think of his campaign whenever they think of him. A crusade never ends, because perfect solutions are never found. But continual pressure is like the squeaky wheel. In a keen house, there are squeaks from all over the place. Every now and then, the government finds itself distracted from its "important" business, and goes out with an oil can. Members who expect quick results are doomed to disappointment. Theories must be tested. The ministry wants to take credit for any progressive moves. The public service is wary of idealistic proposals from politicians. But tenacity and a worthy cause eventually get results, if the Member stays around long enough.

Gerald Baldwin took on the whole establishment when he started his crusade. He wanted to cut down the power of government departments to make new laws by calling them regulations. It all started when he returned from the war, and tried to catch up on the regulations passed while he was away.

"There they stood — volume after volume, shelf upon shelf and row upon row," he says of his visit to the Edmonton law library. "And all these documents, intimately and deeply, had the power to impair the rights, privileges and personal position of ordinary men and women of this country."

None of the regulations was passed by parliament. Many seemed to go far beyond the authority parliament had given. They were dreamed up by someone in a department for his own purposes, and approved routinely by cabinet. And Baldwin was dismayed. "We are years behind other countries which have faced this problem," he said of delegated legislation.

After his election to parliament in 1958, he raised the matter continually in speeches, questions and motion. Nothing happened. In 1964 he struck a responsive note with the Procedure Committee. But they finally decided it was beyond their authority.

By 1968, he had become House Leader of the Official Opposition, and had it in his power to assist or obstruct the government's legislative program. So they threw him a bone, and in September of that year, a special committee was set up to consider the scrutiny of regulations.

In October 1969, the special committee recommended that a permanent committee be set up. That was done. There is now a Standing Committee of the Senate and Commons on regulations and other statutory instruments.

On May 19th, 1971, a bill was passed for better control of regulations. Now, after 13 years, the crusade had resulted in the passage of law. But Baldwin was still not satisfied. In 1973 he introduced another bill to ensure the right of any Canadian to obtain information about government activities.

This is a new phase of his campaign. "We have imposed on the people of this country a bureaucratic jungle," he said in the House. "I have no hope that we will be able to hack it down. But I hope it will be possible to clear out a little space where the ordinary man can stand tall and straight again and see the blue sky."

Other crusades have finally resulted in legislation. My own fight for better pollution control laws, which started in 1964, saw legislation appear in 1970 and 1971. The establishment of a Department of the Environment, and passage of the Canada Water Act, the Northern Waters Protection Act, amendments to the Canada Shipping Act and other laws, are belated moves to meet a real crisis in Canada. But the crusade got things going in the federal House.

Arnold Peters and Frank Howard started a divorce blockade in March of 1960 which finally took routine Quebec and Newfoundland divorces out of the House of Commons. With a push from Bob McCleave in its later stages and over a year's work by a Senate-Commons committee, a new divorce law for all Canada finally emerged in 1968.

Prevention of error is the objective of some crusades. Take Percy Noble, for 15 years a Member from Ontario, who was also a mink rancher. He was worried about the reproductive capacity of the whole human race, and Canadians in particular. Early in 1965 he realized that no baby mink were arriving when they should have. This was a surprise, in view of the well-known habits of mink. Investigation established that their urinary tract and sex organs had been damaged, and 90 per cent of the herd was sterilized. The cause was traced to mink food containing stilbestrol, a fattening hormone. Stilbestrol was used in cattle feed to make them inactive and more easily prepared for market. But some of this drug had somehow got into the mink and had a most undesirable effect on them.

First concerned about his own loss, Percy Noble began to worry about human consumption of meat. How much stilbestrol could be passed to humans, and was it having any effect on them? He started a campaign to find out. He raised the matter time and again by questions to the Ministers of Agriculture and National Health and Welfare. He placed questions on the order paper. He talked about the danger publicly and privately. Tests were conducted. "There is no danger to humans," said the Minister, adding that the use of the hormone would be closely watched.

That wasn't good enough. Use of a synthetic hormone without absolute knowledge of its effect is dangerous. Medical research indicated that diethylstilbestrol (DES) might be a cancer causing agent as well. After an American who had become sterile successfully sued his government for certifying poultry containing DES, it was banned there as poultry feed. But not in Canada.

"Will the government give our people the same protection as 21 other nations that have already banned the use of this material in meat production?" Percy asked John Munro, Minister of National Health and Welfare in May 1972.

"I will have to look into the matter," said the Minister. And he did.

Still banging away at the dangers, Percy Noble retired from Parliament in October 1972. But his campaign succeeded, after 8 years of effort. Effective January 1st, 1973, diethylstilbestrol has been banned for use in the production of food, including beef and poultry in Canada. Percy did his part to keep us all healthy and fertile.

Another Member with a defensive crusade is the Rt. Honourable John Diefenbaker, former Prime Minister. For ten years he has been fighting a rear guard action against government efforts to abolish symbols of the monarchy. Coats of arms, crests and insignia have disappeared. The word "royal" has been dropped. Military regiments with British connections have been disbanded. And it is never done directly. He feels that administrative directives, like the termites he once found boring from within his party, are eating away at the foundations of history. By constant vigilance, the former P.M. makes every move difficult. It is something of a cat-and-mouse game, with the government playing the role of mouse.

Sometimes the crusade is successful, often it is only embarrasing to the government. But the RCMP issue in 1972 and 1973 was both. Following its bilingual policy, the government wanted in some way to get the initials GRC (Gendarmerie Royale du Canada) onto Mounted Police buildings and vehicles. But who everheard of the GRC? The word "police", however, is the same in English and French. So they painted it in large letters on the sides of the Mounties' cars. This meant removing the "Royal Canadian Mounted" part. That made Western Canada very annoyed. From its origins as the North-West Mounted Police, the force has been the special property of the west. Here, in one operation, the East was meddling with western property, the French were cutting into western tradition and the "Royal" was being removed. The force was downgraded to police. It is not hard to guess how western Member Diefenbaker reacted. Well, temporized Prime Minister Trudeau, the big letters would help people recognize the vehicles as police cars. But the angry buzz didn't die down. It was still there on October 30th when Liberal members in the four western provinces dropped from 27 to 7 in the general election. They also lost their one Member in the territories.

In March 1973 new Solicitor General Warren Allmand announced restoration of insignia for vehicles and buildings, very much like the originals. The big "police" letters disappeared.

"Does the minister think there is any danger," asked private Member Diefenbaker, laying a trap, "that Canadians seeing such a car passing by, might not realize that it was a police car?"

"The cars have white doors, with the crest and with RCMP and GRC on them." replied Allmand, dropping right in. "They also have a red light on top and a siren. I doubt that anyone would mistake them for anything else but RCMP cars."

"Does the minister realize," demanded his questioner, "that the Prime Minister said that people would not know it was a police car; and he was afraid guilty criminals would get away?"

No answer.

"Does he recall that?"

Silence.

The crusader settled back into his chair with satisfaction. He now sits waiting for the next mouse to venture forth.

The Donald MacInnis crusade to enforce the rules of debate raised an interesting question. If a Member is given the floor for forty minutes, does he have to talk all the time, or can he just stand there for a while? It started during one of his first speeches. To make sure his remarks were accurate, he wrote them down on a piece of paper. An opposition Member interrupted to complain that he was reading his speech, a practise forbidden by the rules. After putting up a good argument, he was shown where it was written "in the book." So he never read another speech. Nor does anyone else when MacInnis is in his seat. But a lot of people try.

It so happened one day, after he had interrupted several Members, that he was making a speech of his own. An offended speech-reader started hissing. Others joined in. Rather than trying to compete with the noise, MacInnis stopped speaking. The hissing died down. But when he began again, so did the interruption. The second time he stopped, he didn't start again. He just stood there. The Speaker jumped up to ask him to continue, and MacInnis sat down. As soon as the Speaker sat down, he stood up. But he remained silent. The Speaker moved as if to rise.

"There is still some noise over there," MacInnis finally complained. He would not start again until there was absolute silence.

It was a strange House. The Speaker was in the Chair. The clerks were at the table. The reporters were at their desks. Donald MacInnis had the floor, but he wasn't talking. The whole place was in suspended animation except for some faint hissing. Even that shortly faded into mumbled conversation. But he stood his ground. Finally, the House lapsed into total silence, and he finished his remarks uninterrupted. MacInnis has done quite a bit to improve debating manners.

Some crusades are still in progress after many years of effort.

Barry Mathers has had an anti-smoking campaign going since he arrived in parliament in 1962. It has spasmodic success. When Judy LaMarsh was Minister of National Health and Welfare, she quit smoking as an example to Canadians, and started eating instead. John Munro, while Minister, had to do his reduced smoking behind closed doors. But while one department of government is urging Canadians to give up smoking, another is assisting farmers to produce more tobacco. Barry is still trying.

When the 29th parliament met in January 1973, one of the first notices filed was "Mr. Mather, a bill to restrain the use of tobacco."

Heath Macquarrie has been trying for years to have the birthday on January 11th of Canada's first Prime Minister, Sir John A. Macdonald recognized in official fashion. But the fact that Macdonald was also a Tory seems to keep getting in the way. His bill finally reached debating stage in February, 1973, but was thrown into the pot with a bill to commemorate Flag Day, and a bill to commemorate Discovery Day. Committee members of Justice and Legal Affairs were asked to find some way of celebrating all three events, and any others which took place in January, February, or March, on one single holiday. Good luck to them!

David Anderson's 1972 campaign to stop the shipment of Alaska oil by sea down the British Columbia coast came to an end when he left parliament. Others will no doubt pick it up, though it was uphill all the way.

Stanley Knowles wants to abolish the Senate. He has been pressing it for years. He might possibly settle for some drastic reforms. His bill was finally debated for one day in 1973 but then dropped to number 106 on the list. He will have to bring up the subject again in another way.

P.B. "Doc" Rynard campaigns constantly for more attention to the training of medical doctors. "What's the use of spending hundreds of millions on hospitals, medicare and research if there aren't doctors to use them?" he says. But still the government presses on with grandiose social welfare plans without the people to run them. Doc has bothered successive Ministers enough with his questions that they are on the defensive. That augurs well for the future.

Andy Brewin compaigns constantly for better immigration laws. Alf Hales watches like a hawk for evidence of waste and extravagance in government. Tom Bell has been pressing for the establishment of a Canadian merchant marine. Grace MacInnis wants an allowance for non-working mothers, to give recognition to their role in the home. Erik Nielsen is constantly on the alert for scandal or under-handed government activities. Currently he is after security procedures in government, and early in 1973 he submitted six pages of questions for the government to answer.

These crusades have been going on for years. A new Member, John Reynolds, is starting his own campaign to prohibit the killing of polar bears. With persistence he may see results. Other new Members will soon emerge with a crusade firmly attached.

There are many I haven't mentioned. As I said earlier, almost every Member has a crusade. The successful ones are not single-handed endeavours by one Member. Other people often do the ground work, press the issue, and wait in vain. But the focal point is in Parliament. Here a squeaky wheel attracts the attention of press and public, as well as government. Though he seldom gets credit for the final legislation, a crusade gives a Member purpose in life, and satisfaction in a successful result.

THE DISAPPEARING ACT

"The Grand Finale"

It was nearly midnight when Bill Anderson left the council meeting in Galt. It had taken longer than he expected. He glanced at his watch, shrugged his shoulders and got into his car to drive the 300 miles to Ottawa. He had a group to meet and an important committee meeting next day, so there wasn't much alternative. He took a couple of breaks on the way, and the morning light had already appeared when he reached the capital. He didn't feel too bad. After stretching out for a couple of hours, he got through the business of the day.

Late afternoon, it caught up with him. He wasn't really surprised when he suddenly felt weary, so he lay down in his office. But it got worse, and he felt ill. Fellow Member, Dr. P.B. Rynard came down, and he called an ambulance right away.

"This is going to be rough, Bill," he said as the ambulance screamed toward the hospital.

"I know it," replied Bill. But he didn't make it. Before they got him into intensive care, he was dead of a coronary attack.

Bill had been my seatmate, and it was quite a shock for me. It was a great loss for everyone, because he was the friendliest man in the House. Quite apart from his immediate loss, it was a lesson for everyone. If you are over 50, don't drive all night. Thereafter, Members over 50 took care that morning light never caught them driving. Others, of course, didn't feel involved.

Ten other Members of that 24th parliament died in office, all but one of heart attacks. Among them were Sidney E. Smith, former University of Toronto president, and the shining new light of the government as Secretary of State for External Affairs; and Joe Gour who dramatically suffered his fatal attack in the buildings while the House was in session.

The people of Waterloo South elected Gordon Chaplin to fill

the vacancy caused by Bill Anderson's death. But three years later Gordon Chaplin, still their Member, was also dead. He didn't drive late at night. He found other ways.

It's the travelling that does it. Most parliamentary careers end on that account. Not all, of course, wind up so dramatically as Bill Anderson. But the constant struggle, in this gigantic country of Canada, is to get from one place to another without losing working time.

Jack Garland, Minister of National Revenue, finally cleaned up his desk in Ottawa and caught the late train for North Bay. He planned a couple of days on that March weekend in 1964 to see the home town. Having worked till the last minute without eating, he ordered a sandwich on the train. But he felt ill before finishing it. Suddenly he was dead of a heart attack at 46. Jack was a big man, and overweight. But his death came, completely unexpected, at the end of a long week, late at night, and travelling. Five others in that short parliament died without warning.

It was a tough job being chief government whip during the FLQ crisis in late 1970. Things kept going wrong, and Bernie Pilon got the blame. It's the whip's job to see that everybody is in the right place at the right time, but nobody was playing ball. He went home to Beloeil, Quebec for the week-end to try to relax. But he didn't feel well on Monday, so stayed home. On Tuesday, November 17th, he died.

I went to the funeral with a large group of fellow Members. The government provided air transportation. As we left Ottawa, there were military police on hand, reminders of the uneasy feeling of the time. A couple of them accompanied us on the aircraft. But the shock we got on arrival was grim. From the air, it looked as if a battle was in progress. As far as you could see, armed troops were in position. Every road, the airport boundaries, the landing strip, were rimmed with soldiers in battle dress, steel helmets and rifles.

"My God," said Marcel Lambert, "what is this?"

"I guess we're being protected," I said, as we came in for a landing.

Marcel already thought they were overdoing the protection bit. With four years overseas in the armoured corps, he is fairly unflappable. But he well remembered the recent morning when he went out to look at his flower garden, and came face to face with a nervous young soldier, armed to the teeth.

With a heavy escort, we left for the funeral parlour. From there, between rows of soldiers and police, we walked to the beautiful church where the service was held. The army made sure that no politicians were kidnapped or assassinated that day. For many Members, it was the first real contact with the absolute terror that gripped Quebec during that crisis. But it was undoubtedly the most dramatic funeral any Member had in years.

Death in office is not the only result of impaired health. Every election about 20 per cent of the Members decide not to run again. Health is one of the foremost reasons, and heart problems account for the majority of these. I decided not to run in 1972, because heart strain was showing. My Nipissing neighbour Carl Legault, the minister I dogged as critic, Joe Greene, Postmaster General J.P. Coté, Des Code and former minister "Monty" Monteith, all made the same decisions, for the same reason.

We were the lucky ones. The same number of my colleagues in the 28th parliament dropped dead. "Young" Wally Nesbitt suffered a stroke in 1973, then died of a coronary in December. Ches MacRae, Theo Ricard and Harold Winch also left on account of health. And there may have been others among the 52 drop-outs who didn't admit it. A check among these shows most batteries are recharging. For myself, I have recovered to buoyant vitality.

Bud Orange was parliamentary secretary to Resources Minister Joe Greene. Some parliamentary secretaries have nothing to do. But not Bud. Joe gave him jobs, and he did them. When I went to the Bedford Institute in Nova Scotia, Bud was there on behalf of his minister. When I went to the Canadian Water Resources meeting in B.C., Bud was there. He arrived, spoke and left with all the formalities accorded a minister. He went to dozens of other events I never even heard of until they were over. He sat in on committees to guide legislation. He almost had the status of an associate minister. Then one day in 1970, the Prime Minister decided to change the 16 parliamentary secretaries. For Bud and the others, it was devastating. Reduced to desk-pounding back benchers, the spice of life was gone. Bud didn't run in 1972. As a matter of fact, that election saw 7 of those 16 back in private life.

Some ministers give up in mid-career. Edgar Benson's White Paper on Taxation stirred up more Canadians than most tax proposals do. After two years of debate, they became law, with some alterations. Were they his ideas, the Prime Minister's or somebody else's? Cabinet approved them but Benson got the blame. The catalyst for all the anger, he was moved to another department. And when an election was announced, he dropped out, hopefully taking with him, like a magnet, all the tax reform discontent. It didn't work, but Edgar made out all right with appointment as president of the transport commission. Almost the same thing happened to one of his predecessors, Walter Gordon, except that Walter didn't get a job at the end of the rainbow.

Eric Kierans stirred things up in the post office department, trying to make it pay. Dropping a lot of "losing lines" in rural areas, he got plenty of people worked up. In his case they were most certainly his own ideas. He didn't like the government's economic policies either. So he had to go, without compensation.

"It doesn't bother me much getting thrown out of the cabinet," he said "I'd feel worse being late for an appointment." He didn't run in 1972.

Some Members feel they have done their duty. Douglas Harkness was first elected in 1945, following a distinguished military career. His parliamentary career was notable for its iron-firm integrity. Minister of National Defence during the nuclear arms crisis, he would not bend to the Prime Minister when he believed commitments to the Americans should be honoured. Later, he refused to gloss over Lester Pearson's fuzzy explanation of how he misinformed parliament in the Rivard affair. When he spoke, no one ever accused him of improper motives. But after 27 years, he felt he had done his duty.

"A younger person more in tune with present trends can better serve," he said in announcing he would not run. The same idea was expressed by Arthur Laing, minister of veterans affairs.

"Hell, I don't want to be around Ottawa when I'm 72," said Laing.

But he is, for just before the election, he was appointed to the Senate.

Marvin Howe had his wish come true. After 19 years, he decided not to run again.

"Older guys should move on and give younger people a chance," he stated. And a younger person did get a chance. His successor was Perrin Beatty, 22.

By far the greatest majority of drop-outs are disillusioned and fed up with the system. They wait until the end of their term and quietly fade away. Phil Givens was fed up too, but he didn't wait four years, and he didn't go quietly. A former mayor of Toronto, he arrived in Ottawa, believing he had something to contribute. He soon learned that some Prime Ministers don't want help, and don't appreciate suggestions.

"Trudeau told the caucus he liked Members to disagree and criticize," he recalled, "but whenever anyone did, he got the stiletto."

An outspoken man by nature, Givens found that expressing opinions out loud brings no promotion, either."Right then and there I knew I had lost whatever chance I had of corporal stripes," he said after a disagreement with the Prime Minister; and he was right.

But the whole set-up had disillusioned him. "There is no system where an MP with reasonable qualifications can play a useful role," he concluded, "the government is a dinosaur and not responsive to the problems of today." So he resigned in mid-term and ran for the provincial legislature in 1971.

Others are less vocal, and not so fast to decide. But they eventually come to the same conclusions.

While every election finds around 50 Members dropping out, another 50 who want to carry on are defeated. But there are some who like the life, and survive. In former days, politics was a long career for many. Sir Wilfred Laurier had 48 years of public office, 45 years in the House of Commons. Sir John A. Macdonald had 47 years, 24 in the federal House. Some now living had long careers as Members: Earl Rowe with 39 years, Paul Martin with 33 and George McIlraith with 32. But 1973 saw only two long-service Members still in the House; John Diefenbaker with 33 years, and Tommy Douglas who was first elected in 1935, but spent 18 years in the provincial field. To give some idea of the turn-over, only one Liberal who was there when I arrived in 1957 was still there, undefeated, when I left in 1972. That Member was Jean Richard, the humorous, faithful and for 27 years unrewarded Member for Ottawa East. He did not run for re-election, either.

There are some who resign their seats in mid-term. But these people don't drop out of sight. Other duties are awaiting them. There were about 35 during my term. Three, George Pearkes, Paul Comtois and Earl Rowe became Lieutenant Governors of their provinces. Seven became Senators. Eight went into provincial politics and three, Jean Lesage, Ed Schreyer and Frank Moores became premiers. Three, Clem Vincent, Erik Winkler and Hugh Horner became provincial ministers. Seven were appointed to public positions such as ambassadors and commission heads. Two, Erhart Regier and Cy Kennedy, resigned to give their party leader a seat in parliament. Jim Brown was appointed county court judge. Russ MacEwen resigned to accept an appointment as provincial magistrate in Nova Scotia.

"I'm going back to God's country," said Russ, without trying to define Ottawa.

Every election brings a lot of new talent to the House of Commons, renewing and refreshing those who carry on. None of them come in just to stand still in the job. They are willing to serve their apprenticeship, and then on to greater things, like a cabinet position. But that's an illusion for most, which fades as time passes. Though only 1 in 10 are in the cabinet, those odds every Member is prepared for. He can stack himself up against the rest. The problem is, those aren't the real odds. The others are more elusive. First, his party has to get into power or stay in. Then he must come from the right province. A prime minister with 10 superior candidates for cabinet from one province, and only 1 Member who is a dud from another, must pick the dud. The same thing goes for parliamentary secretaries. Once the roster is filled, opportunities are slow in arising.

"How much of an apprenticeship do you serve," asked Phil Givens when he resigned, "before being asked to do something significant?"

He knew the answer already. For some Members, it's forever. What leaders want around them are people they want around. And except for geography, it's their choice.

With all their external worries, Prime Ministers and leaders are plagued with this housekeeping problem. And the more Members they have, the greater the pressures. John Diefenbaker, with

180

over 200 Members, always left some positions unfilled. This was the carrot that kept the boys plodding along. Each thought it was for him, and was encouraged in the idea. Pierre Trudeau tried switching his complement of parliamentary secretries halfway through the term, to give more Members a chance. Neither of these efforts was particularly successful.

The hopefuls go on from parliament to parliament, waiting for their turn in the seats of the mighty. For most it never comes. Some, like those who resign, eventually move to a less competitive arena. Other finally give up.

Quite a few Members drop out because they see their homelife dwindling away, and their profession neglected. Gordon Sullivan, he of the independent mind, expressed it early in 1972 when he decided not to run again.

"I want to spend more time with my family, and return to law," he explained.

Actually, he was appointed a Wentworth County judge, which achieved his goal in a somewhat different way. Jim Lind decided he must spend more time with his family. Paul Gervais, at 47, saw himself at the crossroads.

"I must decide between politics and my profession," he said in March 1972. He chose his profession.

Jack McIntosh had his own reasons. He was discouraged at the constant drift toward socialism. He couldn't even slow it down in his own party. "Is there anybody left at the right-of-centre?" he asked, looking around at his colleagues and seeing very few. After fighting it for 14 years, he finally gave up.

The scene can change very quickly. In my area of Muskoka and Parry Sound, the stage seemed filled with a permanent cast as the seventies began. Frank Miller, local tourist operator, expressed it to me one day in Bracebridge. "I'd really like to get into politics," he said, "but with you in the federal House and Bob Boyer in the Muskoka seat, I don't see any chance for years."

And in Parry Sound, Allister Johnston was almost a fixture in the provincial assembly. But in October, 1971, Bob Boyer decided to return to private life, and the same Frank Miller was elected in his place. In Parry Sound, illness ended Allie Johnston's term, and Lorne Maeck was elected. In October, 1972, I called it quits and Stan Darling took the federal seat. That was a whole new act within one year.

Even if you decide to carry on, and are defeated, all is not lost. After the 1972 election, defeated Members Martin O'Connell and John Roberts were appointed to the Prime Minister's office. Several others became special assistants in Minister's offices; Jerry Pringle in agriculture, Murray McBride in Post Office, Bruce Howard in Health and Welfare and Bob Kaplan in Industry, Trade and Commerce. These fellows only had one four-year term, and found public life fascinating. No doubt the years in the House made them useful and realistic departmental workers. The fact that all are Liberals merely reflects the political facts of life.

Politics is a rough business. Cannibalism is just below the surface. While opposing Members can talk and joke together in the lobbies and corridors, let one trip and fall, and the others are upon him. It's nothing personal, of course. But if he is on the other side, it makes them weaker. And if there is a touch of scandal, it attaches to his party and colleagues. If he is on the same side, nobody adds to his problems. But they don't help too much either. Everybody goes up one in seniority and opportunity for higher office if he slips.

It's rough because it is physically and mentally exhausting. Constant travel, foul-ups, criticism, bad news, tense situations and long hours leave many Members worn out in a very short time. they begin to approach the multitude of problems like approaching a forest at night. It looks like an impenetrable wall rather than a group of trees with vast spaces in between. In the dark they see only an area of unknown dangers. Those who survive best are those with an overwhelming ego, able to walk into that forest with no mental reservation, to lie down in the darkness and sleep soundly without fear, to retrace their steps and start again when daylight comes.

Reluctantly, the Members drifted back to Ottawa at the end of August to legislate an end to the 1973 railway strike. They had hardly got home after the summer adjournment. For many, their first session had seen the glamour fade, and the truth about public life begin to emerge.

"This has been the worst year of my life," admitted new Member Wally Firth as he prepared to return from his home in the Northwest Territories. He had really run to prove that a

182

native Northerner could win. But he hadn't found the prize worth the effort.

"I don't like the weather in Ottawa," he said, "nor the confinement of city life, nor the bureaucratic atmosphere, nor the frustrations of looking after my constituents."

There were others like Wally Firth, but most were still assessing things. They had a new life, sometimes dull, sometimes fascinating; each was a new person, yet still the same; the system was frustrating, yet hopeful; and their constituents were at the same time perverse and loyal.

New Liberal Members in the back seats already felt stifled by their lack of influence. They couldn't know they were far ahead of those who had so recently backed a massive majority. The free vote on capital punishment had given them some liberty. They couldn't know it might be the only one of their career.

All Members had felt the tight thong of the Rules, as they tried to express themselves in their own way. Now they looked forward to some new rules to release the grip. The wiser ones knew better. Slackened in one area, it would tighten in another, unless the whole shape was altered. New Members accepted as natural the fair distribution of House and Committee appointments; the reference of some private Members' bills to committee, and a sense of fair play and accomodation to each other. They could see hard stands and stiff opposition make their mark on government decisions. They were watching a minority government. Maybe, with luck, these new Members forming a third of the House, won't let things slip backwards. Maybe the veterans of past parliaments will back them up in a slow advance to personal freedom. Maybe a new government with a big mandate will be forced to act differently.

But the shadows of the past still lurk in the ranks. As the late summer session began, veteran John Diefenbaker was putting the squeeze on Labour Minister John Munro. When he was called to order the Liberal Members, new and old, knew what to do. They cheered.

"The last thing I want to do is break the rules," said the former Prime Minister with apparent humility.

They didn't believe that. It could only be an act. So they laughed and shouted from the government side.

The moving arms, the staccato chorus and the well-regulated

performance reminded the House veteran of something — circus performers to be exact.

"Ringling Brothers never had such trained seals," he shot back at the noisy crew.

He should know.

Some of the Characters

AIKEN, GORDON, Q.C. The Author. PC Member for Parry Sound Muskoka from 1957 to 1972. He takes a light look at his former colleagues, and finds the expression "trained seals" not too far off. Why then did it take 15 years, 6 elections and a heart attack to get him off the stage? "I guess I'm a slow learner," he admits.

AIKEN, MARIE, The Author's Wife. She managed the home front, filled in at public functions and sighed with relief when it was over. "I'm just not cut out for politics," she said, and went ahead to establish her own reputation in the creative field of crafts.

BELL, THOMAS MILLER, Q.C. "The Whip". Really not as vicious as the name sounds, he wielded the whip with a smile. PC Member for St. John Albert and St. John Lancaster from 1953 to present. Now Opposition House Leader.

CAOUETTE, REAL, "The Boss", Member for Pontiac-Temiscamingue, from 1946 to 1949 and for Villeneuve and Temiscamingue from 1962 to present. Leader of the Social Credit party. The best seal trainer in the business, he gets total loyalty from his Members.

CHAMBERS, EGAN, PC Member for St. Lawrence-St. George from 1958 to 1962. Before election he ran unsuccessfully in 1953, 1954 and 1957. He kept trying, and won.

COWAN, RALPH B. "The Rooster". Liberal Member for Toronto High Park from 1962 to 1968. Named for his strident voice and fighting-cock attitude. The picture was completed by a hank of hair that often stood upright at the back of his head.

DIEFENBAKER, Rt. Hon. JOHN GEORGE, P.C., Q.C., M.A., LL.D. etc. PC Member for Lake Centre 1940 to 1953 and for Prince Albert 1953 to present. Prime Minister from 1957 to 1963. He has the longest record in parliament of any sitting Member. Well biographied, and always good copy. He explains in three words why he once stayed up all night.

DOUGLAS, THOMAS CLEMENT, M.A., LL.D. "Tommy" CCF Member for Weyburn 1935 to 1944; then Provincial Premier; then NDP Member for Burnaby-Coquitlam 1962 to present. Former party leader. Short of stature, but long on wit. When someone shouted "Stand up" as he was speaking, he shot back, "I am. That's my problem. Your problem is from the neck up."

DREW, Hon. GEORGE ALEXANDER, P.C., Q.C., LL.D. PC Member for Carleton 1948 to 1957, after being Premier of Ontario. He was nicknamed "Gorgeous George" by opponents who thought his well-groomed appearance a political disadvantage. He died January 4th, 1973.

DUBROY, J. GORDON, "The Magician", Clerk Assistant of the House of Commons from 1954 to present.

FAIRWEATHER, R. GORDON L., B.C.L. PC Member for Royal and Fundy-Royal 1962 to present. Big, thoughtful and direct, he deplores narrow partisanship and inflexible ideas. But his case for plain talk was frustrated on June 14th, 1972 by a rare Hansard misprint. "I will end with a plea for plaih language and franjnesel3ghl7dealing with l7anl3 ghcreasingly frustrated public" he was reported.

GIVENS, PHILIP GERALD Q.C. "Phil the Lip". Liberal Member for York West from 1968 to 1971. Former Mayor of Toronto. He offered his experience, but it wasn't accepted.

GREGOIRE, GILLES, "The Banty Rooster". Creditiste Member for Lapointe from 1962 to 1968. Short, slight and talkative, he had a lot of Cowan's attributes in a smaller package.

GUAY, JOSEPH-PHILIPPE, "The Happy Heckler". Liberal Member for St. Boniface from 1968 to present. Self-appointed interrupter of Robert Stanfield, he gets back as much as he gives, all in good humour.

HALES, ALFRED D. "The Hawk". PC Member for Wellington from 1957 to present. Chairman of Public Accounts Committee, he keeps a sharp eye for government waste and extravagance.

HEES, Hon. GEORGE HARRIS, P.C. "Gorgeous George II". PC Member for Broadview 1950 to 1963 and for Prince Edward Hastings 1965 to present. Brash (he started his political career by campaigning in army uniform against the Minister of National Defence), a clown "I'd stand on my head in Times Square if it would sell Canadian"; a man's man, a ladies' man. Popular parliamentary performer.

JEWETT, PAULINE, M.A., Ph.D. Liberal Member for Northumberland from 1963 to 1965. She was a professor of political science at Carleton University. Interviewed for this book, she admitted: (a) the stories recorded, (b) several others, (c) politics is a lot different in fact than in class, and (d) she would like to write a book, too.

KENNEDY, CYRIL F. "Cy". PC Member for Colchester-Hants from 1957 to 1967. His courage included severing his own shattered arm during the war, and 20 years later severing his own political career to give his Leader a seat in parliament.

KIERANS, Hon. ERIC WILLIAMS P.C. Liberal Member for Duvernay from 1968 to 1972. Salesman, economist, teacher, provincial minister, stock market president and federal minister, he created a storm wherever he went. "I like controversy," he says.

KNOWLES, STANLEY, B.D., LL.D. "The Holy Ghost". (what else would you expect for a gaunt clergyman) NDP Member for Winnipeg North Centre from 1942 to 1958 and 1962 to present. He also earns the nickname for his short sermons to the House on the Rules.

LAMBERT, Hon. MARCEL, P.C. B.Com. M.A. "The Instant Expert". PC Member for Edmonton West from 1957 to present. He has total recall of parliamentary matters. While Speaker of the 25th Parliament, he enforced the rules firmly. Becoming a private Member again, he delayed asking questions. "We decided he couldn't think of one he would have allowed as Speaker," comments Barry Mather. The silence was temporary.

LAMOUREUX, Hon. LUCIEN, Q.C., M.A., L.Ph. Member for Stormont and Stormont-Dundas since 1962. Deputy Speaker 1963 to 1965. Speaker of the House of Commons 1966 to present. He is patient, firm, humourous and human; but his daily wrangle with the Members for recognition at the question period leaves many of them vexed. It's constantly on his mind. Lloyd Crouse was recently introducing this former Member Aiken, who had changed a bit. "Do you recognize this fellow?" he asked. "Much easier than in the House," was the Speaker's quick reply.

LEWIS, DAVID, Q.C. "Tight Rope Walker", Member for York South 1962-63 and 1965 to present. Leader of the New democrats. He likes to be incisive, with both feet on the ground. But fate, in the form of the 1972 election, left him up in the air.

MACDONALD, DAVID, PC Member for Prince and Egmont from 1965 to present. This David is ready to tackle any over-fed goliath. He has an ulcer, which he constantly feeds with turmoil. After clergyman David had "concluded" one speech several times, Arnold Peters announced, "Let us pray."

MACDONALD, Hon. DONALD STOVER, P.C., LL.M. Liberal Member for Rosedale from 1962 to present. Big, bustling and bellicose, he delights in authority. But underneath beats a human heart, which he sometimes displays.

MACDONALD, FLORA, PC Member for Kingston and the Islands from 1972 to present. In 1973 the Mounties searched her office for missing Indian affairs documents, making her the only Member suspected of siding with the Indians.

MACQUARRIE, HEATH NELSON, B.A., M.A. "The Professor". Member for Queens and Hillsborough from 1957 to present. A witty intellectual with a broad range of interests. In one day he could dissect a theory of political science and then protest a report on superior American dental standards. "Canadian mouths should be as clean as American mouths," he declared.

MARTIN, Hon. PAUL, P.C., Q.C., M.A., LL.D. etc. "The Strategist". Liberal Member for Essex East from 1935 to 1968. He's been around the political course so often he knows every bump and crevice. "We both know it's a game, so let's play it well." Presently government Leader in the Senate.

OTTO STEVEN, "The Reluctant Rebel" Liberal Member for York East from 1962 to 1972. He looked tough, he talked tough. But he couldn't desert.

PEARSON, Rt. Hon. LESTER BOWLES, P.C., O.B.E., LL.D. etc. Member for Algoma East from 1948 to 1968. Prime Minister from 1963 to 1968. His experience in futile world politics left its mark in his "let it be" attitude. Sweet reason, generosity and unsupervised delegation of authority brought situations where disloyalty was impossible. So he accomplished a lot without ever having a majority. Died December 26, 1972.

PEPIN, Hon. JEAN-LUC, P.C., L.Ph. "Smiley". Liberal Member for Drummond from 1963 to 1972. A university professor of invariable good humour. He was occasionally a bit ruffled when English-speaking Members mispronouced his name. He didn't mind John Luke Peepin, or Gene Luck Pippin, but "Don't call me John Leak Poopin". Sometimes it's the little things that cause racial strain.

PETERS, W. ARNOLD, NDP Member for Timiskaming from 1957 to present. He is Northern Ontario's man from Missouri; he doesn't believe anything. Even the "act of God" clause in labour and insurance contracts is fixed. "God is never on my side in those contracts," he complains, "but always on the side of the companies."

PICKERSGILL, Hon. JOHN WHITNEY P.C., M.A. Called "jumping Jack" from his constant jumping up to object, and his jerky movements. Member for Bonavista-Twillingate from 1953 to 1968. He had a successful career as senior civil servant, author, Member and minister. Having a quick mind, he sometimes spoke before he thought. "If he were crossing a ten acre field with 25 clow-flaps in it," quipped critic Diefenbaker, "he'd manage to step in all of them."

RYNARD, PHILIP BERNARD, M.D., C.M. "Doc". Member for Simcoe East and North from 1957 to present. Everybody's doctor on parliament hill. From waitresses to prime minister, he runs a one-man free first aid service; and is health critic to boot.

SECRETARIES — LILLIAN "BILLIE" GRAY and AMELIA COLE, make appearances here and there. Billie Gray rode herd on thousands of departmental and riding problems for 12 years; when she left Ottawa she rounded up another expert, Amelia Cole. Between them, they kept one Member out of trouble. Billie Gray also typed the manuscript.

STANFIELD, Hon. ROBERT LORNE, P.C., Q.C., LL.D. etc. PC Member for Colchester-Hants and Halifax from 1967 to present, after being Premier of Nova Scotia. Well biographied by Geoff. Stevens and others. Has great ability to unify, assess and act positively at the proper time. Some Members thought him slow when he first arrived in 1967 with his careful speech and deliberate actions. They should have looked more carefully.

THOMPSON, ROBERT NORMAN, B.Sc. Member for Red Deer from 1962 to 1972. He was national Leader of the Social Credit Party. With Réal Caouette as deputy leader, he was a draft horse harnessed to a racer. Break-up of the Western party took him to the Conservatives in 1968.

TRUDEAU, Rt. Hon. PIERRE ELLIOT, P.C., Q.C., LL.L. etc. Liberal Member for Mount Royal from 1965. Prime Minister of Canada 1968 to present. Well biographied. He brought informality to the office, which Canadians initially welcomed. Some Members thought him a freak when he first arrived in 1965 with his unconventional clothes and aloof manner. They sneaked over to the government lobby to have a look. Here again, they should have looked more closely.

WOOLLIAMS, ELDON, Q.C., LL.B. "The Audible Orator". PC Member for Bow River and Calgary North from 1958 to present. He has positive views, and nobody has seriously asked him to speak up.

PLUS a supporting cast of over 200.

NOT INCLUDED in the text were hundreds of good friends and interesting characters whose witty sayings got edited (not censored) out.

ALISTAIR FRASER, Clerk of the House, and ERIK SPICER, Parliamentary Librarian were helpful with information, but bear no responsibility for the result.